TO THE WORK YOU LOVE

an Interactive Study

DAN MILLER

48 DAYS

TO THE WORK YOU LOVE

an Interactive Study

BROADMAN
& HOLMAN
PUBLISHERS

NASHVILLE, TENNESSEE

Ten-digit ISBN: 0-8054-4373-8
Thirteen-digit ISBN: 978-0-8054-4373-8

Published by Broadman & Holman Publishers
Nashville, Tennessee

Dewey Decimal Classification: 248.84
Subject Headings: CHRISTIAN LIFE \ VOCATIONAL GUIDANCE

Unless otherwise noted, Scripture quotations have been taken from the Holman Christian Standard Bible®, copyright © 1999, 2000, 2002, 2003 by Holman Bible Publishers.

Other Scripture quotations are KJV, King James Version of the Bible and TLB, the Living Bible, © Tyndale House Publishers, Wheaton, Ill., 1971, used by permission.

This publication is designed to provide accurate and authoritative information with regard to the subject matter covered. It is provided with the understanding that the publisher is not engaged in rendering legal, accounting, or other professional advice. If legal advice or other expert professional assistance is required, the services of a competent professional person should be sought.

——From a Declaration of Principles jointly adopted by a Committee of the American Bar Association and a Committee of Publishers & Associations

1 2 3 4 5 6 7 8 9 10   10 09 08 07 06 05

The Purpose of *48 Days to the Work You Love Interactive Guide* is to train and equip you to understand yourself, recognize new opportunities in the workplace, create a plan, and move with confidence to higher levels of success and accomplishment.

OVERVIEW OF *48 DAYS TO THE WORK YOU LOVE*

48 Days to the Work You Love is a strategic program designed to help you move ahead in your career with the confidence, boldness, and enthusiasm that only comes from having clear personal understanding and a clear plan of action. When we hear that 70 percent of Americans would change jobs if they could, it raises some questions: Are there that many bad jobs out there? Why with unemployment critically low are there still people doing something they don't enjoy? In a job seeker's market why isn't everyone moving quickly to what gives them the most fulfillment? The answer is that most people have not taken the time to look at themselves before choosing a job or a career. They simply choose the job based on chance opportunity, income potential, or others' expectations. Thus they live lives of quiet desperation and often "go to their graves with their music still in them" (Henry Ward Beecher). What a tragedy in the time of greatest opportunity in history!

48 Days to the Work You Love is an extensive but flexible program. It deals with the "whole person" rather than sets of skills or compartments of knowledge. 85 percent of the process of having confidence of proper direction comes from looking inward first. The more you can know about yourself, the more confidence you can have in moving forward. Responding to only external circumstances leaves one vulnerable. With that frame of reference, any obstacle can send you in a new direction. It is only by knowing oneself thoroughly that you can then have the confidence in making proper life decisions. *48 Days to the Work You Love* is a foundation for successful living and learning that can be the starting point for confident decisions in work, family, and social environments. You can move through the exercises gaining self-understanding, a clearer sense of calling or purpose, and then seeing the applications in daily fulfilling work.

SETTING A TIME SCHEDULE

This program is divided into 5 primary sections requiring 2 to 3 hours each. These may be structured in a way that best meets your needs or requirements. Those 5 sections are further divided for a total of 12 segments. Structure your time so you can digest the principles rather than just lightly read them.

Possibilities would include:

1. Five sessions—perhaps working on the same weeknight for each of five weeks. This has traditionally been the most advantageous arrangement for assimilation of the material.

2. Five sessions where you dedicate Monday through Friday night of the same week. This is a fast pace and would require a fair amount of time each day. It is workable if you are not currently working.

3. Twelve one-hour sessions. You may be able to do this as a group with others in a Sunday school schedule or an academic class. It's easy to make this work as each section has multiple assignments.

4. A single day process. This does not allow for working through the assignments and allows only a cursory look at some of the components.

SUPPLEMENTARY MATERIALS

To supplement your *48 Days to the Work You Love* materials, references will be made to additional articles and resources. They will also stimulate more understanding of the issues. The audio CDs included with this program are not just a verbal reading of the workbook material. They include real-life examples and encouragement to help you integrate this into a life plan.

This process encompasses more than just filling in the blanks. Traditional career materials have superimposed vocations or jobs on people. This material moves from the inside out. Only as you understand your uniqueness can you then move forward confidently. And that is an individualized process.

Your preparation for these working sessions, your enthusiasm and your belief in the process will set the stage for the results you will ultimately see. Yes, the world may seem to be an unfair place and bosses and spouses can be demanding and unrealistic. But in reality the world is basically a fair place, and we tend to get compensated accordingly. Also, people tend to end up pretty much where they expect to end up, so see yourself in the driver's seat at each step of this process.

Table of Contents

A NOTE FROM DAN

Early in life we begin the process of determining what we want to be when we grow up. Our first and most obvious options often are doctor, lawyer, merchant, chief. However, reality sometimes hits our options head-on. Changes in technology, transportation, and communications are eliminating and opening new career opportunities at this very moment.

All of these factors may provide frustration, discouragement, excitement, and hope all at the same time. Each of us will respond differently. The challenges are to:

1. Be ready to respond because the changes are inevitable.

2. Know yourself so completely that there will be a sense of continuity even as the changes occur around you.

As you work through this process, be encouraged! There is hope! The options today are limitless. You really can be prepared, focused, and ready to move forward with the confidence, boldness, and enthusiasm that project you into the next opportunity.

In this workbook you will have the opportunity to explore the changes, understand yourself, go through the traditional steps of finding a career and also look at the expanding area of nontraditional work.

Complete each step, filling in the blanks and making your own notes. This is an individualized process. It is your life, and this is your process. Answer each question honestly, and it will guide you to clear patterns that identify the right plan of action for you. Stick to a time schedule. Don't procrastinate! Review the *48 Days* schedule on the next page of this book right now and put yourself on track for the success you deserve.

Please inform us of your results or how we can improve this process. Expect success!

Your friend in the process,

Dan

READY TO START? THE 48 DAY SCHEDULE

Here's where the rubber meets the road. Put yourself on this time schedule so you can turn your dreams into goals. Work through each step and keep moving even if you feel you could do more work on a particular step.

Each day's assignment refers to a section of the workbook. You may want to do a quick overview and read some of the examples of people who have dramatically changed their success level. This is a step-by-step process to get you through one of those inevitable transition points in your life. Learn how to do the process, and it will serve you again and again.

You'll notice there is an aggressive reading/introspection section in the first couple of days. This is meant to get you quickly through to the actual job change steps. If you are just evaluating at this point, you may want to take more time on these first four sections.

Check off each day's activities as you complete them. See yourself getting closer and closer to the work you love!

_____ Day 1   Understand Change—
                      Prepare for the Future   Pages 1–16

Review the statistics on workplace change. Complete the questions listed in this section. Recognize that with any change there are the equal seeds of opportunity.

_____ Days 2–3   Define Clear Direction
                      (5-Year Goals)   Pages 17–44

As you identify the Life you want, you will begin to recognize the work that you were meant to do. Your life will not be meaningful without making deposits of success in 7 different areas of your life.

_____ Days 4–5   Assess Personal Skills and Abilities,
                      Personality Tendencies, Values,
                      Dreams, and Passions   Pages 45–56

Your work options go far beyond what you have the ability to do. The more you know about yourself the more confidence you will have about choosing the right work environment.

_____ Day 6   Create Personal Mission Statement
                                              Page 121

Relax and reflect on what you know about yourself. Now you can create a personalized picture of your goals. Every great company has a Mission Statement. See yourself as a great company. What unique skills and goals need to be included for your life to make a difference? What will define a life well lived? Working is about much more than just earning a paycheck. Take advantage of this time to see a bigger picture of your life.

_____ Day 7   Design Résumé   Pages 62–65

Now you have laid a foundation and can move toward the application for your life. Review the material in this section and create or update your résumé. Make sure it does more than just give a chronological snapshot of what you've done. You want your resume to be a sales brochure for you and to position you as a great candidate for what you want to do.

_____ Day 8   Make Résumé Copies (50)

On nice white, ivory, or tan paper with matching blank pages for your introductory and cover letters.

_____ Days 9–10   Create Target List of Companies
                    to Be Contacted   Pages 84–85

Spend two hours with your city directory or a national business search engine where you can get a brief company history and profile and the names of proper contact people.

_____ Days 11–12   Compose Introductory and
                    Cover Letters   Pages 84–85

Use the example given for your format on pages 128–29.

_____ Day 13   Send 15 to 20 Introductory Letters
                    Step 1   Pages 84–85

_____ Day 17   Send 15to 20 Résumés and Cover Letters
                    Step 2   Pages 84–85

Send second 15 to 20 introductory letters.

_____ Days 21–22   Begin Phone Follow-up on First Résumés
                    Step 3   Pages 84–85

Remember how critical this is. Your statistical odds of getting a job offer just from sending out résumés is 1 out of 254. Add an actual phone contact to that, and it drops to 1 out of 15!

_____ Day 24   Send Second Set of 15 to 20
                    Résumés and Cover Letters

You're halfway there. This is Day 24 of the 48. You've made a lot of progress. Stay positive! Remember this is a process. You are taking the initiative in contacting companies. You will contact some organizations that can't use you and don't know why you contacted them. But this is the way we find the 87 percent of those unadvertised positions. And this is how you bypass competitors, putting yourself in position for the best and most exciting opportunities.

_____ Days 28–29   Phone Follow-up on Second Set of Résumés

_____ Days 24–35   Schedule Interviews   Page 85

Review "8 Reasons Why You Are Not Getting a Job Offer!" on page 120. Practice, practice, practice. Review information on Interviewing. Ask for the interview. No one cares about your success more than you do. Make sure you stay in the driver's seat all the way through this process.

_____ Days 35–40   Second Interviews—Negotiating Salaries
                                                          Pages 105–109

Review helpful Internet sites for salary ranges see page 130. Be sharp, enthusiastic, and confident. Once they want you and you want them, you are in a position to negotiate with confidence.

_____ Days 40–47   Evaluate and Make Decisions

Ask for more information. Talk to people already working in prospective companies. Make any follow-up contacts from previous prospects where a decision had not been made. Remember, things change quickly, and you have created "top of mind" positioning with many companies. You can do a quick review of any possibilities that you stirred up.

_____ Day 48   Make Your Decision

Commit to the focused, fulfilling, and directed choice. See this as the next "season" of your life. Your new job is one tool for a successful life. Make sure you are continuing to make deposits of success in other areas of your life as well.

Check these items off as completed. Stay on track with this short but intensely focused process.

Section 1

Is All Change Good?

1. Yes, change is challenging. But we also know that with any change, there are always the equal seeds of opportunity.

2. We are all confronted with change. No one can choose to avoid it. Our only choice is how are we going to respond. Are we going to be victims or victors? Whiners or winners?

3. Everyone has obstacles. Someone is too old, too young, too short, does not have a college education, is from the wrong ethnic group, or is disabled. In this process we are going to look at assets, not liabilities. Most of these things are in reality obstacles between our own two ears more than to a world desperate for competent workers.

Chapter One

The Challenge of Change

From 1920 until the mid 1980s, getting a job with some large company was the dream of most every young American. The unwritten agreement between the corporation and the employee was: *If you work for us throughout your working lifetime, we will take care of you.* I still hear rare stories where someone has worked at a company for thirty-two years, or at least had a mom or dad who did.

Then in the 1980s this system rapidly disintegrated. Twenty million blue-collar workers, many of whom had spent their entire lives working for one organization, were let go. What happened? Fifty years ago it took a lifetime for technology to make your job irrelevant—now it takes just 4 to 5 years. Experts estimate that 80 percent of all products and services we are currently using will be obsolete in five years. Here in middle Tennessee hundreds of manufacturing and apparel companies have disappeared as manual labor positions are moved abroad. Many of you reading this may have already experienced firsthand the effects of moving from a production to a knowledge-based economy.

We are also told that 50 percent of all the jobs we will have in the next 6 years have not yet been created. StaffMark, the large national temporary-staffing agency, predicts that in the next 4 years, 50 percent of the work force will be contract, or contingency, labor. These changes require that each of us develop a clear sense of who we are and where we are going. Otherwise we will feel victimized by the inevitable changes.

- *Time* magazine noted that in a recent survey approximately 1.2 million jobs were eliminated, or 3,287 every day.
- 70 percent of American workers experience stress-related illnesses.
- 34 percent think they will burn out on the job in the next 2 years.
- The *Los Angeles Times* reports that there is a 33-percent increase in heart attacks on Monday mornings.
- According to the national Centers for Disease Control and Prevention, more people die at 9 o'clock Monday morning than any other time of day or any other day of the week.
- *Entrepreneur* magazine adds that there is a 25-percent increase in work-related injuries on Mondays.
- Male suicides are highest on Sunday nights, with men realizing that their careers—and possibly their finances as well—are not where they want them.

NOBODY GETS FIRED ANYMORE

In a recent workshop, we were hearing from the many participants who were recently "released" from their jobs. The terms for being "let go" became the center of attention as we moved around the room. It seems no one just plain gets "fired" anymore in this politically correct work environment.

In 1980 a person got "fired." By 1985 it was "laid off." In 1990 it became "downsized." Now a person can be "rightsized," "restructured," "reorganized," "reengineered," or "put in the mobility pool." I hear that many people are being freed up to "pursue other opportunities." In this computer age, some people are being "uninstalled" and receiving their termination notices via e-mail.

The coldest term I have heard recently is that certain people are informed that they are "surplus." Isn't that a nice feeling after 25 years of faithful service? You are essentially in the same category as the 16 cases of Liquid Paper now that we have spell-checker.

Is it surprising that morale is often low for the remaining employees who realize that their workload has tripled, their salary has remained the same, and they are the "lucky" ones to be around after all the smart ones took the buy-out package and immediately got better jobs elsewhere? Now we have to redefine lucky.

Some Bureau of Labor Predictions through 2010 (as of March 2005):

- The service-producing sector will continue to be the dominant employment generator in the economy, adding 20.5 million jobs by 2010.
- As employment in the service-producing sector increases by 19 percent, manufacturing employment is expected to increase by only 3 percent over the 2000–2010 period. Manufacturing will return to its 1990 employment level of 19.1 million, but its share of total jobs is expected to decline from 13 percent in 2000 to 11 percent in 2010.
- Health services, business services, social services, and engineering, management, and related services are expected to account for almost 1 of every 2 wage and salary jobs added to the economy during the 2000–2010 period.
- Office and administrative support occupations are projected to grow more slowly than average, reflecting long-term trends in office automation. Production occupations should grow much more slowly than average because of advances in manufacturing technology.
- Eight of the 10 fastest growing occupations are computer related, commonly referred to as information technology occupations.

The good news is that small businesses are adding more than 2 million new positions annually, far outweighing the traditional job losses. Yes, these jobs may look different; they may not come with a company car, 401(k), and a medical plan; but they are exciting new opportunities. These companies don't have to comply with many of the federal regulations that often mandate companies with fifty or more employees. They may be harder to find, but this is where the growth of opportunities lie.

SMALL BUSINESS AND JOB GENERATION

- Small businesses represent over 99 percent of all employers in America (Small Business Answer Card, Small Business Administration).

- Small business creates 80 percent of all new jobs in America (State of Small Business, the Small Business Administration).
- During national recessions of the economy, small business appears to be almost the sole source of job growth (*A Small Business Primer*, William J. Dennis Jr., The NFIB Education Foundation).
- From 1988 to 1990 small businesses with fewer than twenty employees accounted for 4.1 million net new jobs, while large firms with more than 500 employees lost 501,000 net jobs (*A Small Business Primer*, William J. Dennis Jr., The NFIB Education Foundation).
- Today, 52.8 percent of the companies in America employ fewer than five people; nearly 90 percent employ fewer than twenty workers. Only 2.6 percent have more than 99 employees. (*A Small Business Primer*, William J. Dennis Jr., The NFIB Education Foundation).

Your best opportunity may not look like your last job. A position with a small company may not have a fixed salary, a company car, a pension plan, or medical benefits. But it may in fact be a great "fit" and true opportunity for you.

How would you describe the season of life you are in currently? What are its major opportunities and challenges?

_____

_____

_____

Who gave you your first job? What kind of job was it? How much money did you make?

_____

_____

_____

 ## DO YOU WANT TO BE A BUTTERFLY OR A FREAK?

A man found a cocoon of a butterfly. One day a small opening appeared. He sat and watched the butterfly for several hours as it struggled to force its body through that little hole. Then it seemed to stop making any progress. It appeared as if it had gotten as far as it could, and it could go no further. So the man decided to help the butterfly. He took a pair of scissors and snipped off the remaining bit of the cocoon. The butterfly then emerged easily. But it had a swollen body and small, shriveled wings. The man continued to watch the butterfly because he expected that at any moment the wings would enlarge and expand to be able to support the body, which would contract in time. Neither happened! Instead the butterfly spent the rest of its life crawling around with a swollen body and shriveled wings. It never was able to fly. What the man, in his kindness and haste, did not understand was that the restricting cocoon and the struggle required for the butterfly to get through the tiny opening were God's way of forcing fluid from the body of the butterfly into its wings, so that it would be ready for flight once it achieved its freedom from the cocoon.

Sometimes struggles are what we need in our lives. If God allowed us to go through life without any obstacles, it would cripple us. We would not be as strong as what we could have been. We could never fly!

If you look at your work life so far, what has the greatest value or worth?

_____

_____

_____

Describe a time when you were forced into an unwanted or unexpected work change.

_____

_____

_____

What would be the key characteristics of an ideal job?

_____

_____

_____

_____

If nothing changed in your life over the next five years, would that be OK? What are you willing to change in order to get new results?

_____

_____

_____

 ## BLACK CRABS—BE ONE AND DIE!

In his book *Rich Dad, Poor Dad,* Robert Kiyosake tells the story of the Hawaiian Black Crabs. If you go down to the beach early in the morning, you can find black crabs. You can put them in your bucket and continue walking on the beach. Now those crabs start thinking, *We are bumping around in this little bucket making a lot of noise but going nowhere.* Eventually, one crab looks up and thinks, *There's a whole new world up there. If I could just get my foot up over the edge, I could get out, get my freedom, and see the world in my own way.* So he stretches up, pushes a little, and sure enough, gets one foot over the edge. But just as he is about to tip the balance and go over the edge, a crab from the bottom of the bucket reaches up and pulls him back down. Instead of encouraging him and seeing how they could help one another get to freedom one by one, they pull anyone attempting to get out back down into that confining bucket where death will come quickly.

Unfortunately, many of us live around a bunch of black crabs, ready to ridicule any new idea we have and just as eager to pull us back down to their level of performance. I have found that one of the key characteristics of successful people is that they hang around people who are performing at the level at which they want to perform. There will always be naysayers and whiners; avoid them. Find winners and spend time with them!

Companies are restructuring, reengineering, outsourcing, and redefining the way we think.

Everyone lives on the edge of job obsolescence and the threshold of career opportunity. We have long been told that with every change there is the seed of new opportunity. Yes, not all change is positive growth, but all positive growth does require change. Change is the common thread in the history of mankind. It is predictable and inevitable, impersonal and relentless. The quickening pace is touching everyone. The question is not will change reach you, but how will you respond?

Our strategy needs to focus on handling the change process and turning it into a positive force.

How do you respond to change? Do you see it as providing new opportunities or as a threat to expected security? What is "security"? Is it a guaranteed future? A company that provides medical benefits, vacation time, and a retirement plan? Not anymore. Security today is not likely to come from a job, a company, or the government. General Douglas MacArthur said, "Security is your ability to produce."

Your only "security" is knowing what you do well. Knowing your *areas of competence* will give you freedom and remove any vulnerability from corporate politics and unexpected layoffs.

> *"The factory of the future will have only two employees, a man and a dog. The man will be there to feed the dog. The dog will be there to keep the man from touching the equipment."*
> —Warren Bennis, author and distinguished professor of business administration, University of Southern California

Briefly describe your current work situation.

_____

_____

_____

How did you get involved in this occupation?

_____

_____

_____

Why would you consider a job/career change at this time?

_____

_____

_____

Wayne Gretsky was asked why he was such a great hockey player. He responded with an eloquent morsel of wisdom: "I simply went to where the puck *was going to be*." An average player would see the puck and go toward it.

BEGIN THE LIFE YOU WANT TODAY!

I heard a story from my friend Bob Whitley about an old dog lying on the front porch. A neighbor approached the porch and could hear the dog softly moaning. He asked his friend why the dog was whimpering. The owner said, "He's lying on a nail." Predictably the man said, "Well, why doesn't he move?" To which the owner replied, "I guess it doesn't hurt that much yet."

I find a lot of people like that old dog. They moan and groan about their situation but don't do anything. How bad does the pain have to be before you get up and do something else? In the workplace today there are incredible opportunities. If you are in a negative environment, one that causes you pain and anguish, maybe it's time to take a fresh look at yourself, define where you want to be, and develop a clear plan of action for getting there.

For tips on how to take advantage of new opportunities, check out other information at www.48Days.com.

Are there any issues other than your work causing unrest? If so, what are they?

_____

_____

_____

How much of your wanting change is motivated by a desire to increase your income?

_____

_____

_____

"Obstacles are those frightful things you see when you take your eye off the goal."—Hannah More, quoted in *Multiple Streams of Income,* by Robert G. Allen

DEALING WITH OBSTACLES IN OUR PATH

In ancient times, a king, wanting to test his subjects, placed a boulder in the main road leading to his city. Then he hid himself and watched to see people's reactions. Some of the king's wealthiest merchants and courtiers came by and simply walked around it. Many loudly blamed the king for not keeping the roads clear. None did anything about getting the big stone out of the way. Then a peasant came along, carrying a load of vegetables. On approaching the boulder, the peasant laid down his burden and tried to move the stone to the side of the road. After much pushing and straining, he finally succeeded. As the peasant picked up his load of vegetables, he noticed a purse lying in the road where the boulder had been. The purse contained many gold coins and a note from the king, indicating that the gold was for the person who removed the boulder from the roadway. The peasant learned what many others never understand: taking initiative presents unexpected rewards.

Chapter Two

Common Career Questions

1. Should I find one job and stay with it until I retire?

The average job in America now lasts 3.2 years. The average American worker will have 14 to 16 different jobs. You must develop a sense of what you can contribute that goes beyond just 1 company or organization. A career path today will likely involve moving from organization to organization, creating a picture of rising circles, rather than a vertical ladder. In fact, a vertical rise within one organization will likely move you away from your strongest areas of competence.

Is this rapid rate of change intimidating to you? _____ Would you prefer to have one job and stay with that company forever? _____

2. Do I have to deal with change?

Change is inevitable. It is relentless and nondiscriminating. Our only choice is how we are going to respond to it. If you know your strongest competencies, are prepared, and have a clear focus, you will have a sense of continuity so there is no feeling of starting over each time you are confronted with a job change.

The only way you can deal with relentless change is to know what is changeless about you. What are your nonchanging strongest abilities?

_____

_____

3. How can I keep my job from controlling my life?

First decide what kind of life you want, then plan your work around that life. Make sure you build in balanced priorities. Exchange your time for valued priorities, not just money. Move away from the idea that more time equals more success. Many ideas don't even equate to more time equals more money. If you are working more than 45 to 50 hours a week in your job, you are surely limiting success in some other areas of your life. Don't expect all your fulfillment, value, and meaning to come just from the work you do. Make sure you are making deposits of success in all 7 areas of your life. (See chapter 4: The Power of Having a Goal.)

How many hours have you been working? _____ Does that allow time for deposits of success in other areas of your life? _____ Do you understand that more time does not necessarily mean more money or more success? _____

4. What if I don't want another corporate job? Do I have other options?

Many people are switching to their own businesses. It was estimated that by the end of 2004, 60 percent of American homes were housing some kind of business. In the next 5 years that number will grow dramatically. There are many choices for businesses you can run yourself. (See section 5: Nontraditional Work.) In addition, there are many subtle varieties of work models available today: consultants, freelance workers, temps, independent contractors, etc.

Have you been able to see the new kinds of opportunity all around you?

_____

What are 3 or 4 ideas you've had that have the potential to add or replace your current income?

_____

5. I don't have a college education. What can I do?

Recognize that 85 percent of the reasons people get promotions, advancements, and opportunities in companies are due to personal skills—attitude, enthusiasm, self-discipline, and interpersonal ability. Only 15 percent is due to technical or educational skills and credentials. Today's work environment creates a level playing field. If you have the personal skills, you can do most anything you want. (See chapter 6: Understanding My Personal Characteristics.)

What are your 15 percent assets?

_____

_____

How would you describe your 85 percent assets?

_____

_____

_____

6. I am sending out résumés to every job that appeals to me in the paper but get no response. Is there something else I should do?

Only about 12 percent of the positions available ever appear in the paper. Learn how to find the jobs before they are in the paper. The major difference between a successful job hunter and an unsuccessful job-hunter is not education, age, skill, or ability, but the way he goes about his job search. (See chapter 8: Creative Job Search Strategy.)

What system have you used in the past to find jobs or opportunities? _____

_____

7. My résumé forces me into a rut that I can't seem to get out of. What can I do?

Build your résumé, highlighting your transferable areas of competence, not just a list of job descriptions. Show things like administration, planning, sales, marketing, training, supervising, financial analysis, etc. as areas of proficiency. These skills are transferable from 1 industry or profession to another. (See chapter 7: Shaping the Options.)

Is your resume just a historical overview of your work? Do you believe it positions you for moving to your best opportunity? _____

_____

I repeatedly see anger, frustration, and bitterness over a job loss. While it's not unexpected, it also becomes counterproductive quickly. Most anger is transparent, and I've seen people sabotage their best efforts of going through the motions of a new job search. Recognize that the past company is not suffering because of your anger; you are. Break the cycle by seeing yourself in the driver's seat in creating the future you want.

How has a company change affected you? How did it make you feel? _____

_____

What would be the key characteristics of an ideal job/career? _____

_____

So what are you doing while you're unemployed? One good idea is all you need to change your life!

Don't just stop with the thought, *I wish I had invented Monopoly, but that's been done and there will never be another similar opportunity*. Actually, we are seeing an explosion of new board games. Seattle waiter Rob Angel came up with "Pictionary" and went on to sell 40 million copies; then came "TriBond," "Take Off," and "Cranium." Having the idea is of little value, but acting on it can change your life. Most people get stuck in the thinking stage and never get to the acting part.

 ## SO WHAT ARE YOU DOING WHILE YOU'RE UNEMPLOYED?

In 1934, Charles B. Darrow of Germantown, Pennsylvania, was unemployed. To amuse himself and pass the time, he created a board game that provided the possibility of fame and fortune. That game is called "Monopoly." Today, it's the best-selling board game in the world, sold in 80 countries and produced in 26 languages including Croatian.

Incidentally, he originally presented it to the executives at Parker Brothers, but they rejected the game due to "52 design errors"! But Mr. Darrow wasn't daunted. Like many other Americans who have been unemployed, his situation and personal passion for the game inspired him to produce it on his own.

With help from a friend who was a printer, Mr. Darrow sold 5,000 handmade sets of the game to a Philadelphia department store. People loved it! But as demand grew, he couldn't keep up with all the orders and came back to talk to Parker Brothers again. The rest, as they say, is history! In its first year, 1935, the "Monopoly" game was the best-selling game in America. And over its 70-year history, an estimated 500 million people have played!

• Over 200 million games have been sold worldwide.
• More than 5 billion little green houses have been "built" since 1935.
• The longest game in history lasted 70 straight days.

SOMETIMES YOU GOTTA LET GO OF THE PEANUTS!

George has been with the same company for twenty-three years. He hates his job, changing in and out of his uniform at the office to avoid having his neighbors identify him in that role. He has missed much of his children's lives, works on his wife's day off, and his health is deteriorating. He is knowledgeable in computer programming, and friends frequently ask him about setting up their home and business systems. But he can't imagine leaving the security of his job.

Now let me tell you how they catch monkeys in Africa. The natives take a coconut and cut one end off to make a small hole just large enough for a monkey's hand to enter. The other end of the coconut is attached to a long rope. They then carve out the inside of the coconut and put a few peanuts inside. They place the coconut in a clearing and hide in the trees with the end of the rope. The monkeys come around, smell the peanuts and reach inside to grab a fistful. But now, with a fistful, their hand is too large to retract through the small hole. Then the natives yank on the cord and haul that silly monkey to captivity because the monkey will not let go of those few lousy peanuts he thought he wanted.

What idea have you had where you failed to act but then saw someone else make it a reality?

_____

_____

What are two or three ideas you may have now that could be developed? _____

_____

Thousands of ideas can be developed for meaningful work outside the traditional job.

COMMON QUESTIONS
- Is this really all there is?
- Am I doing what God wants me to do?
- Does my life have a purpose?
- Did I make a wrong turn somewhere?

Everyone lives on the edge of job obsolescence and on the threshold of career opportunity.

Change is the common thread in the history of mankind. It is predictable and inevitable, impersonal and relentless. The quickening pace is touching everyone. Here's the challenge: be prepared to respond.

The key to power in our careers is first to look at ourselves.

The more we understand ourselves, the more we can move forward with boldness and confidence. We enhance our effectiveness by first being introspective.

> "Know thyself, and to thine own self be true."
> —Shakespeare

> "Until you make peace with who you are, you will never be content with what you have."
> —Doris Mortman

What were your childhood goals and ambitions for life? Which ones have you been able to fulfill?

_____

_____

When you daydream, what do you see yourself doing?

_____

_____

_____

What have been the happiest, most fulfilling moments in your life? _____

_____

_____

Who are two or three people you know who seem to have accomplished their dreams in life? What do you remember about their accomplishments? _____

_____

_____

Money is ultimately never enough compensation for doing a job.

There must be a sense of purpose, meaning, and accomplishment.

When you look at your personal life, what have you done that you consider to have the greatest value? _____

_____

Just because you have the *ability* to do something does not mean that it is well-suited for you. This is a significant point that cannot be stressed enough. Many people have been misdirected because they had the

> *"The unexamined life is not worth living."*
> —Socrates

> *"The secret of success is focus of purpose."*
> —Thomas Edison

 ## WHAT ARE YOU GOING TO BE WHEN YOU GROW UP?

When you get to heaven, God is not going to ask you why you weren't more like Mother Teresa. He's likely to ask you why you weren't more like you. Your responsibility and source of real freedom and success is to discover who you are. Lead with your own unique talents and personality. Be authentically you and let God use you.

The most common comment I hear from job changers is "I still don't know what I want to be when I grow up." While this is usually said with an embarrassed humor, it's not an unreasonable position. The process of finding one's purpose and path is an ongoing process. It's not something you do one time at eighteen years of age and then forget. Your life experience helps you clarify as you go; and with your own maturity and the changes in the work environment, you are a different candidate now than you were 20 years ago, regardless of your age today. Look for your unique path for this season in your life.

HOW TO STOP WANTING WHAT I WANT

Here's a recent question I received: *"Dan, I'm writing you because I have a question that I haven't been able to find an answer for. I've looked through the bookstore for something on the subject but to no avail. You are good at helping people figure out how to achieve what they want, not only in careers but more importantly in life. What I need to know is how to stop wanting those things that I want for my life? No one else can seem to help me. Can you?"*

I will not share my personal answer to this person, but, believe me, this is either a painful or a misguided question. What do you think? How do you stop wanting those things that you want? How do we become numb to the desires of our hearts? And is that a reasonable goal? Should I just find a job that pays the bills and try to forget doing something I really enjoy? I think not! My response is to clarify what you want, create a plan of action, and begin to walk toward that goal, unashamedly, never wavering.

The power of knowing yourself acts as a compass through change. Popular writer Stephen Covey says the only way we can handle change around us is to know what is *changeless* about ourselves.

Doing things faster or more efficiently is not the goal if you are not doing the right things. Finding a job is a meaningless process until you develop a clear focus that is suited to you.

---

ability to do something well. At this stage in your life, you probably have the ability to succeed at 400 to 500 different things career-wise.

Dennis is a 43-year-old dentist. Last year he made more than $300,000 in income. His practice is growing, and his "success" is reflected in his beautiful house and the vacations he and his family are able to take. However, he is also being treated for depression and is increasingly overtaken by panic attacks and the dread of going to the office. In working through this process, we discovered that while Dennis has the ability to be a dentist, he is living out his parents' dream, not his own. He has now sold his dental practice and has gone back to school to get his degree in family counseling.

Rather than the panic of feeling fired, downsized, or uninstalled, perhaps you or someone you know has been given the gift of "the grace of interruption."

"ALL BEGINNINGS ARE HOPEFUL!"

The president of Oxford University spoke these words to the entering freshman in 1944 in the midst of a world war. This is a concept that we have seen confirmed throughout history. In working with people going through change, I am often struck by the discouragement, frustration, and frequent anger and resentment. I have come to recognize, however, that those feelings always tell me that the person is looking backward—at something that has already occurred. As soon as we are able to create a clear plan for the future, those feelings quickly begin to dissipate and are replaced by hope, optimism, and enthusiasm. In all my years of coaching, I have never seen a person who has a clear plan and goals who is also depressed. They just don't go together.

Viktor Frankl, in his wonderful little book *Man's Search for Meaning*, relates his observations of people in the German concentration camps. Age, health, education, or ability could not predict those

> *Genius is the ability to clearly visualize the objective.*

who survived the atrocities there. Only those who believed that there was something better coming tomorrow were able to survive and ultimately walk away from those camps.

Feeling discouraged? Miserable in your job? Just lost your business? Give yourself a new beginning tomorrow! "All beginnings are hopeful."

What could you do to create a new "beginning" in your life today? _____

_____

_____

Setting positive goals is often more about what you will stop doing than in adding new things to do. What are two things you'd like to stop doing? _____

_____

_____

TAKEAWAYS

1. No one is in this process alone.
2. There is hope for the future. Today is a time of tremendous opportunity.
3. You can do this!

REFLECTIONS ON WORK MATERIAL

1. Review chapter 1, "The Challenge of Change." Think through your own history.
2. Review chapter 2, "Common Career Questions." Which of these questions have you already lived through?
3. Talk through the questions in chapter 2. Then write answers to all the questions.

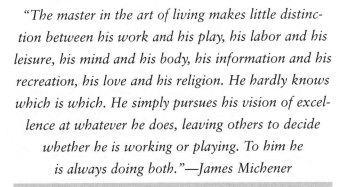

"The master in the art of living makes little distinction between his work and his play, his labor and his leisure, his mind and his body, his information and his recreation, his love and his religion. He hardly knows which is which. He simply pursues his vision of excellence at whatever he does, leaving others to decide whether he is working or playing. To him he is always doing both."—James Michener

 ## THE GRACE OF INTERRUPTION

This phrase was reported recently by a lady who had been laid off unexpectedly. She related that she had been given "the grace of interruption." If we look at those words, it really does imply a very positive occurrence. *Grace* is defined as "an attractive quality," "the condition of being favored," or even "a short prayer in which a blessing is asked." Surely any of these are to be desired. An *interruption* is "a break in the continuity" or "an intermission." Think of the intermission of a game where players review what has happened and then plan for better results and more success in the second half. These together seem to set the stage for a refreshing pause to become newly focused and energized.

Rather than the panic of feeling fired, downsized, or uninstalled, perhaps you or someone you know has been given the gift of the grace of interruption.

ASSIGNMENTS FOR NEXT SESSION

1. Complete creating a life plan (chapter 3).
2. Rate yourself on the Wheel of Balance (chapter 3).
3. Complete the five-year goals section (chapter 4).
4. Listen to the first half of CD 1.

48 DAYS
Hall of Fame

Jim had a music degree from a highly respected, prestigious university. With that degree he had been able to build a reputation as an independent composer/arranger and was viewed as a success by all who knew him. However, Jim was frustrated with the volatility of the music industry and tired of what he saw as backstabbing and disloyalty.

In working through the process of life planning with Jim, it became clear that the one thing he enjoyed more than anything else was being on the water. He understood sailing and had even bought and sold a few boats. When it was suggested that he make boating the focus of his career, Jim was at first incredulous: how could he possibly do what he enjoyed more than anything else in the world and still provide for his family?

Jim was assisted in refocusing his résumé so it would not pigeonhole him in the music industry but rather highlight his skills in organization and customer service. He followed that with a 10-day, in-person job search through the Carolinas, visiting only those few towns where he would most like to live. Two weeks after making those contacts, Jim experienced an incredible 3 days. On Monday morning he received a call offering him a position in Charleston, South Carolina. On Tuesday, he received a call offering him a position in Washington, North Carolina. On Wednesday, he was called from a company in Oriental, North Carolina, offering him a position there. All were reputable boat dealers, wanting him to join them in their sales and promotional efforts. Faced with the enjoyable task of choosing between 3 dream positions, Jim and his family moved to Charleston and began living out his dream life.

(See www.48Days.com.)

Section II

What Do I Want to Be When I Grow Up?

1. In our society, we tend to plan our lives around our work. The focus of this entire program is to learn how to plan your work around the life you want.
2. Life balance is critical. Extreme *success* in one area will likely borrow success from another. We want to identify and build toward true success in all seven areas of life.
3. Without a goal, we will drift through life. We are in danger of becoming what Zig Ziglar calls "wandering generalities." Nobody becomes a success by just drifting. Clear goals do not restrict us; rather they release us to freedom and accomplishment.

Chapter Three

Creating a Life Plan

WHAT ARE WE REALLY WORKING FOR?

Sometimes success is seeing what we already have in a new light.

An American businessman was at the pier of a small coastal Mexican village when a small boat with just one fisherman docked. Inside the small boat were several large yellow-fin tuna. The American complimented the Mexican on the quality of his fish and asked how long it took to catch them.

The Mexican replied, "Only a little while." The American then asked why he didn't stay out longer and catch more fish. The Mexican said he had enough to support his family's immediate needs.

The American then asked, "But what do you do with the rest of your time?"

The Mexican fisherman said, "I sleep late, fish a little, play with my children, take a siesta with my wife, Maria, stroll into the village each evening where I sip wine and play guitar with my amigos. I have a full and busy life."

The American scoffed, "I'm a Harvard MBA, and I could help you. You should spend more time fishing and with the proceeds buy a bigger boat. With the proceeds from the bigger boat, you could buy several boats. Eventually you would have a fleet of fishing boats. Instead of selling your catch to a middleman, you would sell directly to the processor, eventually opening your own cannery. You would control the product, processing, and distribution. You would need to leave this small coastal fishing village and move to Mexico City, then Los Angeles, and eventually New York City where you will run your expanding enterprise."

The Mexican fisherman asked, "But, how long will all this take?" To which the American replied, "15 to 20 years."

"But what then?"

The American laughed and said, "That's the best part. When the time is right, you would announce an IPO and sell your company stock to the public and become very rich. You would make millions."

"Millions? Then what?" the native fisherman asked.

"Then you could retire. Move to a small coastal fishing village where you would sleep late, fish a little, play with your kids, take a siesta with your wife, and stroll to the village in the evenings where you could sip wine and play your guitar with your amigos." (I've borrowed from this story that's been circulating in many forms—Author is unknown.)

> "And in the end, it's not the years in your life that count. It's the
> life in your years."—Abraham Lincoln

Do you really need to build bigger barns or have you been overlooking the real success you already have? _____

_____

_____

What are the things you are already doing that you want to continue until you die?

_____

_____

_____

> "The journey of discovery consists not in going to new lands,
> but in having new eyes."

Most Americans evaluate their lives in retrospect, having no clear sense of control, purpose, or destiny for the future. Without knowing where you are going, you are doomed to evaluate your life in retrospect.

Here are some unsolicited but revealing statements about where people see themselves:

- 51-year-old businessman—"I feel like I've lived my whole life by accident."
- 34-year-old CPA—"I feel like a prostitute. In return for a nice salary, they've taken my heart, soul, and mind."
- Wife of professor—"I feel like we have been free-falling for the last 13 years."
- Salesman—"I feel like I'm a ball in a pinball machine."
- 56-year-old PhD in theology currently driving a bus—"I feel like I've been given six seconds to sing, and I'm singing the wrong song."
- 53-year-old businessman—"I feel like my life is a movie that's almost over, and I haven't even bought the popcorn yet."
- Collection agent—"I've lived my life up until now as though driving with the parking brake on."

- 46-year-old "successful" car salesman—"I feel like a lost ball in tall cotton."
- 39-year-old automotive engineer—"I'm a butterfly caught in a spider's web, with my life slowly being sucked out."
- 27-year-old computer specialist—"I'm a box of parts and nothing fits together."
- 31-year-old attorney—"Law school sucked all the life and creativity out of me."
- 32-year-old in family business—"The merry-go-round of my professional life has left me no farther than a few steps from where I got on and with a weak stomach."

> *"Life is never made unbearable by circumstances, but only by lack of meaning and purpose."*
> —*Victor Frankl*

These are frequent feelings among even "successful" people. It is common to reach that point in life where you need to take a fresh look at what you are doing and where you are going.

What phrase would describe your current life situation? _____

_____

_____

What phrase would describe your ideal position in life? _____

_____

_____

_____

A clear sense of purpose will provide a feeling of continuity and contentment to carry you through those inevitable changes. Developing a clear focus leads to confidence, boldness, and enthusiasm in living out that focus. Those who cannot define a desired future are doomed to repeat the past. If you cannot visualize what you want the future to be, you are likely to end up feeling like a victim of circumstances. And we know that if you want different results, you must change what you are doing. In fact, *insanity* is defined as continuing to do the same things and expecting different results.

LEARNING TO GET BACK UP

When a baby giraffe is born, within a few seconds it struggles to its feet. Shortly afterward, however, the mother will knock it over from its wobbly stance. This process is repeated each time the baby struggles to its feet until the young giraffe has the strength to stand on its own without falling. What seems like an unkind act is, in fact, of vital importance to the survival of the young animal. It is an act of love by the mother for her child. For the baby giraffe, the world is a dangerous place and it must learn without delay how to quickly get back on its feet.

The late Irving Stone, who spent a lifetime studying the lives of great men such as Michelangelo, Vincent van Gogh, Sigmund Freud, and Charles Darwin, noted a common characteristic of all great men: "You cannot destroy these people," he said. "Every time they're knocked down, they stand up."

(Adapted from "Illustrations for Preaching & Teaching" from *Leadership Journal,* by Craig B. Larson.)

"I LOATHE MY WORK!"

I hear a lot of poignant phrases as people describe their work. This happens to have come from a young attorney. Loathe is not your common everyday word. Webster defines it as "to feel intense dislike, disgust, or hatred for; abhor, detest." Obviously, it's pretty difficult to put yourself into your work if you loathe it. There may be attempts to perform as others expect you to and you may even be able to do the basics and get a paycheck. But you are not likely to experience meaning, purpose, peace, or fulfillment in work you loathe.

Now interestingly enough, the first Webster definition for work is this: "bodily or mental effort exerted to do or make something; purposeful activity." So you may hate your job, but by definition you aren't "working" (purposeful activity) if you are doing something you hate. Maybe we can come up with a new word for people who spend their time doing something they hate: e.g. lifeblotcher, wasteahololic, insaniac, shortsighter. Help me out here. . . .

You can recognize that you hate your job today, but if you stay there, you will begin to see deterioration in other areas of your life—physical, emotional, spiritual, and in your relationships. This process will help you create a plan for success in each of those areas.

If you know where you are going, you can respond to *priorities* rather than *circumstances*. Develop a long-term perspective; don't be like the farmer in Aesop's fable "The Goose and the Golden Egg." The farmer, having become impatient with getting only 1 golden egg a day, decided to cut the goose open and get all the eggs at once. Obviously, not understanding the anatomy of a goose, he cut off the opportunity to get anymore golden eggs. We are in a society that emphasizes instant everything: microwaves, fax machines, cell phones, and instant coffee. Real personal success seldom comes not in that instant fashion but by careful planning for the long-term future.

When we talk about success, we are talking about balance and success in more areas of life than just career and finances. Too many people have sacrificed success in one area for success in another. Stay committed to achieving success in multiple areas of your life.

Describe a time when a specific pain in your life prevented you from seeing anything else.

_____

_____

_____

_____

Going through job change provides a great opportunity to take a fresh look at your success in other areas. Rather than seeing your life at a standstill, see the opportunities for increasing your success in areas other than work. Make additional deposits of success in your physical well-being. The energy and creativity that can come from a sharp mind and body can generate the ideas you need at this time. Take the kids to Taco Bell rather than to O'Charley's and enjoy the time together. Organize a pot luck with a group of your friends—you'll be surprised how many of them are going through a similar experience, and providing one dish will cost you no more than eating your own meal. Pick up a great book to read. If you read only 10 minutes a day, you can read a new book a month—and that can transform your insight and preparation for new options. Stay connected spiritually. You'll realize that in the scope of eternity, this event is probably a tiny spot on the time line.

Our common American model has been:

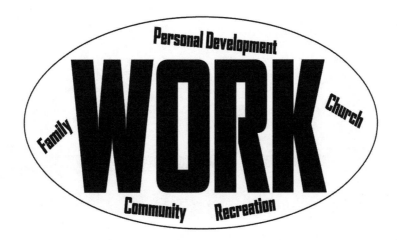

In this model, the job is central. We are frequently more defined by *what we do* than by *who we are*. When meeting a new person, the conversation normally goes as follows: "Hi, John, I'm Dan. What do you do?" From that one brief answer, we make conclusions about that person's intelligence, education, income, and value to society. With this model, we get our total sense of worth from our work. All other aspects of our lives are forced to fit in around the job . . . if there is time. This leads to resentment, frustration, feelings of loss of control and lack of balance. It also leaves one vulnerable in that if something happens to that job, whether by circumstances or by your own choice, then the question becomes, "Who am I?" That is what happens when your total identity and sense of worth are in your job.

How would you describe your current focus on work? _____

_____

_____

_____

 ## A MAN WITH A TOOTHACHE

Shakespeare once wrote, "A man with a toothache cannot be in love," meaning simply that the attention demanded by the toothache doesn't allow him to notice anything other than his pain. In working with people going through job change, I often find Shakespeare's principle to be confirmed. I see grown men ignoring their wives, hiding out to avoid seeing their friends, watching too much TV, and eating foods that blunt their minds. I see women, embarrassed about yet another layoff, stop going to church, spend money they do not have, read romance novels rather than inspirational material, and snap at their kids when asked an innocent question. The "pain" of the job seems to mask the health, vitality, and success they have in other life areas.

Can you imagine a life where your work was not the absolute center of your life?

_____

_____

_____

What we need is a paradigm shift to:

Work   Family

Recreation   Community   Church

Personal Development

Yes, your *job-work-vocation-career* has to incorporate how God has gifted you, what you want to accomplish, and how you want to be remembered. However, you need success equally in those other areas as well. You need a *life plan* with balance, not just a *job*. Remember, a job is simply one tool for a successful life.

Our goal is to help you:

Plan your *work* around your life rather than planning your *life* around your work.

What hobbies do you have? What other skills and interests do you have? _____

_____

_____

_____

What gifts and talents do you have that have never been used in your work? _____

_____

_____

_____

How are you involved in your community? _____

_____

_____

THE RAT RACE—IMPROVE YOUR LIFE; THINK LIKE A RAT

We talk about "being in the rat race," but this is probably unfair. It's actually demeaning to the rats. Rats won't stay in a race when it's obvious that there's no cheese. The popular little book *Who Moved My Cheese?* showed how even smart rats quickly look for new routes to follow when the cheese is gone. Humans, on the other hand, seem to get themselves into traps from which they never escape. Some research shows that up to 70 percent of white-collar workers are unhappy with their jobs. Ironically, they are also spending more and more time working.

Jan Halper, a Palo Alto psychologist, has spent 10 years exploring the careers and emotions of more than 4,000 male executives. He found that 58 percent of those in middle management felt they had wasted many years of their lives struggling to achieve their goals. They were bitter about the many sacrifices they had made during those years.

Rats, however, move on once they realize the cheese is gone or perhaps was never there. Rats would probably be embarrassed to be labeled "being in the human race" for doing ridiculous things like continuing to go to a job that they hated every day.

By looking at these areas other than career, one can develop clear patterns and commonalties that then help define what, in fact, the career/job/business/vocation ought to be. This really is a reverse process but one that leads to true fulfillment. Too often, people choose a career or line of work because Uncle Bob did it or because they heard that you could make a lot of money doing it.

The measure of a man is not what he does on Sunday but rather who he is Monday through Saturday.

"OUR CAREERS KEPT US APART"

I rarely purchase the sensational magazines in the grocery checkout lane. This time I made an exception. The front cover of *US Weekly* had the headline: "Tom and Nicole Separate—'Our Careers Kept Us Apart.'" Give me a break! Do they have to keep their work schedules to make the mortgage payment? No, this is just an extreme example of misplaced priorities! Here's a quote from the article: "Citing the difficulties inherent in divergent careers which constantly keep them apart, they concluded that an amicable separation seemed best for both of them at this time." Yeah, explain that to the 8- and 6-year-old children. "Kids, Mommy and Daddy think having a great career is more important than being a family."

With all the options today, it is critical to define your own priorities. If you simply respond to circumstances, any obstacle will send you in a new direction. Circumstances should not determine our choices. Well thought-out priorities can guide us through the inevitable changes that will come our way. Careers are tools for successful lives but nothing more than one piece of a successful life. Without success in finances, family, socially, physically, spiritually, and in personal development, career success will be empty and meaningless.

I JUST WORK FOR THE MONEY

"Law school sucked all the life and creativity out of me." "I've never been happy practicing law." "I have never had a sense of purpose." "I feel destined to do something great but have no idea why or what." "I work only for the money."

These are statements from a young attorney who in his last position had been sick for 6 months, "triggered initially by stress." But a new "career opportunity" presented itself, and he is now working in a prestigious position with a Fortune 500 company. Unfortunately, the sickness is returning, starting with the symptoms of a choking feeling and shortness of breath.

Ultimately, money is never enough compensation for investing our time and energy. There must be a sense of meaning, purpose, and accomplishment. Anything that does not blend our values, dreams, and passions will cause us to choke on some level. Events of the last two years have caused all of us to reassess what's important. A life well lived must go beyond just making a paycheck, even if it's a large one.

The Bible tells us in Ecclesiastes 5:10; "Whoever loves money never has money enough; whoever loves wealth is never satisfied with his income." If money is the only reward of your job, you will begin to see deterioration in other areas of your life—physically, emotionally, spiritually, and in your relationships. Need a new plan? (See www.48days.com/personal_coaching.php.)

Are you chasing "cheese" that is no longer there? If so, why?_____

_____

_____

_____

- Recognize that your career is not your life. It is simply one tool for a successful life.
- Don't put all your energies into one area. Be committed to achieving success in all 7 life areas.
- Our physical health has a direct relationship to the energy and creativity we bring to our work.

"That every man find pleasure in his work— this is a gift of God." (Eccles. 3:13)

- Our career success directly impacts our finances.
- Our success in finances and the other areas will never far exceed our personal and spiritual development.

Write briefly about your father's or mother's attitude toward work and how that has affected you. _____

_____

_____

A Dream plus a Detailed Plan of Action—Create a New Future.

A plan of action will separate you from 97 percent of the people you meet. Everyone has dreams, but few ever turn those into goals. The difference between a dream and a goal is that a goal is a dream with a time frame of action attached.

The Wheel of My Life

My Areas for Achievement

Each of the categories in the wheel on the next page represents a composite of our lives. Rate yourself by shading in each section to the degree you are reaching success in that category. (A score of 10 is great, while a score of 1 puts you at the center of the wheel and means you need some work.)

You know what an out-of-balance wheel will do. A life out of balance feels much the same. No one wants to be the guy in the hospital with a heart attack even if he has $5 million in the bank. And no one wants to be in great physical shape but rejected by family and friends. You cannot justify success in one area at the expense of success in another area. Make the decision now to have success in all 7 areas.

> *"Goals serve as a stimulus to life. They tend to tap the deeper resources and draw out of life its best. Where there are no goals, neither will there be significant accomplishments. There will only be existence."—Anonymous*

 ## LIVING MY DREAMS

Recently in working with a young man, he expressed this sentiment: "My fear is that I will discover what I love doing but by then be too old to enjoy a full life of living it out." Wow, what an approach/avoidance conflict. Remember those from your introductory psychology classes? You want a cookie but know that if you reach for it your hand will get slapped.

What about this above stated fear? When do you cross the line age-wise where it's just better not to want or know about a better life, but better just to exist and wait for the grave? Is it 35, 50, or 70? Is ignorance really bliss after all? I've had 27-year-olds who are fearful that they've missed the window of opportunity for a life well lived. If your dream was to play quarterback in the Super Bowl, that may be true, but for most of us, living out our dreams is not 1 event.

Look for recurring themes in things that get your attention. Is it art, music, children, old people, cars, caring and nurturing, birds, reading, flying? Don't think that your dream needs to be new and revolutionary. We all know someone like Susie who sells seashells by the seashore, but most lives of fulfillment may look ordinary to an observer. We find that even those who end up extremely wealthy are not necessarily doing something rare; rather the critical element is that they are doing something they truly enjoy!

Your dream life will integrate your (1) skills and abilities, (2) your personality traits, and (3) your values, dreams, and passions. Trust your heart in this process. It's more intuition than logic. Be confident you can live out your dreams. Don't settle for less!

Just as you make financial deposits and withdrawals, you do exactly the same thing in all these other areas. Learn to recognize when you are making a "withdrawal" or a "deposit" physically, spiritually, in personal development, etc.

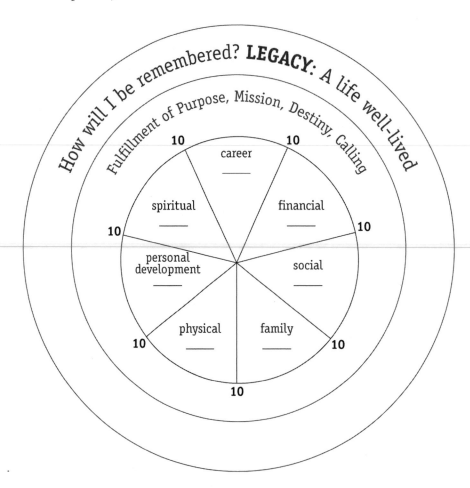

Without deep and clearly defined goals of your own in each of these areas, the activities of your life will reflect the desires of those around you. Recognize that your success in all 7 areas will determine the ultimate fulfillment of your *purpose, mission, destiny,* and *calling.* Those will build the *legacy* you leave behind.

What does your wheel look like? Would it roll smoothly, or would it provide a lumpy ride?

_____

_____

_____

_____

Chapter Four

The Power of Having a Goal

If nothing changed in your life over the next five years, would that be OK? _____

_____

_____

_____

If you want different results next year, what are you willing to change in what you are doing

now? _____

_____

_____

_____

There is considerable evidence to indicate that expectations of your future do, in fact, tend to create your future. Dr. Paul Yonggi Cho, pastor of the largest church in the world, says:

"What you have in your heart becomes your experience."

People usually end up pretty much where they expect to end up.

It seems reasonable, then, to spend some time determining specific, worthwhile expectations that will make your life more meaningful. Keep in mind that only about 8 percent of the general population can identify clear goals and only about 3 percent ever actually write those down. I'm talking about specific goals, not just the "I want a bigger house and a nicer car" variety. With this process, you can quickly put yourself into the 3 percent category, and trust me, it is widely known that those 3 percent ultimately accomplish more than the remaining 97 percent.

The best way to predict your future is to create it.

Are you a goalsetter? Do you typically set goals at the first of the year? If not, why not?

_____

_____

_____

Remember, in this career/life-planning process you will be identifying your:

1. **skills and abilities,**
2. **personality traits,**
3. **values, dreams, and passions**

As you integrate these into realistic areas of opportunity well suited to you, it will be necessary to consolidate them into goals. The following process will help you get an initial focus. You may feel you are being rushed or hurried.

> *"With definite goals you release your own power, and things start happening."—Zig Ziglar*

However, you will find that if you do not begin to make decisions, you will tend to procrastinate and your history will simply repeat itself. A quick decision is often the best decision and is certainly better than no decision. And you might want to be reminded that the current definition of *insanity* is to keep doing what you've always done and expect different results.

Indecision is the greatest thief of opportunity.

Goals are not written in concrete and unchangeable terms but certainly give you a starting point and a destination. The important thing is that you are working on your goals; your life has meaning only when you are working toward worthwhile goals.

Success:
The progressive realization of worthwhile goals.

 MASTER GARDENER OF YOUR SOUL

Our minds are like gardens; they grow whatever we allow to take root.

"Just as a gardener cultivates his plot, keeping it free from weeds, and growing the flowers and fruits, which he requires, so may a man tend the garden of his mind, weeding out all the wrong, useless, and impure thoughts, and cultivating toward perfection the flowers and fruits of right, useful, and pure thoughts. By pursuing this process, a man sooner or later discovers that he is the master gardener of his soul, the director of his life. He also reveals, within himself, the laws of thought, and understands, with ever-increasing accuracy, how the thought-forces and mind-elements operate in the shaping of his character, circumstances, and destiny." (*As A Man Thinketh* by James Allen)

Control your own destiny by controlling what goes into your mind. The books you read, the thoughts you think, the television you watch, the conversations you participate in, the people you associate with, and the music you listen to combine to create your future. Are you sowing the seeds for the life you want 5 years from now?

For your purpose in life to be fulfilled, you must set goals in multiple areas. Success is not just career-related or financial; family, physical, and spiritual areas are equally important aspects of achievement. They are part of the same whole. This is the whole-person concept of the *48 Days to the Work You Love®* approach.

Time is the only resource you can never recapture. Are you spending or investing your time?

WHERE AM I NOW? PERSONAL CHECKUP

1. Am I missing anything in my life right now that's important to me? __ YES __ NO
2. I know what I am passionate about. __ YES __ NO
3. I am well organized, know how to focus on my top priorities, and get a lot done every day. __ YES __ NO
4. I have a written, strategic plan for my work and personal life with time lines and quantifiable measurements. __ YES __ NO
5. I have ample time for my family and social relationships and feel good about the balance I have achieved. __ YES __ NO
6. I exercise 4 to 5 times a week to restore myself physically. __ YES __ NO
7. I am regularly achieving my income goals. __ YES __ NO
8. My life reflects my spiritual values, and I am growing, maturing, and gaining wisdom in this area. __ YES __ NO
9. I have studied and developed the new, creative ideas I have had this past year. __ YES __ NO
10. I believe I am fulfilling my mission in life. __ YES __ NO

GOAL-SETTING WORKSHEET

Any stage in life can be an exciting time with many opportunities or a dreary time of confusion and entrapment. You may not be able to change your circumstances, but you can decide that the circumstances won't dominate you. You do have choices.

A goal is a dream with a time frame on it.

WORK IS LOVE MADE VISIBLE

Here are some of Kahlil Gibran's thoughts on finding the work you love:

Work is love made visible.

And if you cannot work with love but only with distaste, it is better that you should leave your work and sit at the gate of the temple and take alms of those who work with joy.

For if you bake bread with indifference, you bake a bitter bread that feeds but half man's hunger.

And if you grudge the crushing of the grapes, your grudge distills a poison in the wine.

And if you sing though as angels, and love not the singing, you muffle man's ears to the voices of the day and the voices of the night.

All work is empty save when there is love;

And when you work with love you bind yourself to yourself, and to one another, and to God.

Begin with the five-year goals and then work backward to what you need to do today to make deposits in what you want to be five years from now. Be specific, creating quantifiable benchmarks to track your deposits of success.

Something magical happens when you write down your goals. I have seen people transform their levels of success almost instantly simply as a result of getting clearly defined and written goals.

LIFE BALANCE—LIFELONG LEARNING AND SUCCESS IN SEVEN LIFE AREAS

Theme verse: 3 John 1:2
Dear friend, I pray that you may prosper in every way and be in good health, just as your soul prospers.

Here are the seven essential areas for success:

1. FINANCIAL: INCOME, INVESTMENTS

In Malachi 3:10–11, the real financial principle—does God just promise to meet our needs? "Take delight in the LORD, and He will give you your heart's desires" (Ps. 37:4).

Don't let *failure* cripple you. "If thou faint in the day of adversity, thy strength is small" (Prov. 24:10 KJV).

"Make no small plans; they have no magic to stir men's souls."—Daniel Burnam

Beginning Today!	*One-Year Goals*	*Five-Year Goals*

How much do you want to be earning each year in 5 years?_____

_____

_____

_____

What part does generating income play? Be specific here. Don't think that it is just being materialistic or self-centered. If you are a faithful steward of resources God allows you to control, what would you like to flow through you to bless others?

How much do you want to have in the bank or in investments?_____

_____

_____

_____

If you can't dream it, it won't happen! Nothing is unrealistic if you have a clear plan. What can you do today to make a deposit in the financial success you want?

_____

_____

_____

I will save _____ percent of my income each week.
I will give _____ percent to _____.
I will increase my income by $_____ or by _____ percent in the next 12 months?
Be Specific _____
How can we measure this? _____
Make it personal:
• I earn _____.
• I drive _____.
• I invest _____.

2. PHYSICAL: HEALTH, APPEARANCE, EXERCISE

Recognize the power of feeling great. An energized body can enhance your creativity and ability to "see" new opportunities.

> "Now may the God of peace Himself sanctify you completely. And
> may your spirit, soul, and body be kept sound and blameless for
> the coming of our Lord Jesus Christ." (1 Thess. 5:23)

Beginning Today!	*One-Year Goals*	*Five-Year Goals*

"The feeling of being hurried is not usually the result of living a full life and having no time. It is, on the contrary, born of a vague fear that we are wasting our life. When we do not do the one thing we ought to do, we have no time for anything else—we are the busiest people in the world."—Eric Hoffer

Do you take long walks, exercise, or meditate regularly? _____
_____
_____
_____

Are you living a balanced life? Is this an area that deserves more time?_____
_____
_____
_____

Can you give yourself just 30 minutes to relax?_____
_____
_____
_____

Have you recently experienced physical exercise as a cleansing process that dramatically increased your creativity? _____
_____
_____
_____

Wealth is difficult to enjoy if you've given up health in the process.
- I exercise _____ times weekly doing _____.
- I get _____ hours of sleep each night _____.
- I enjoy vitality, health, and energy because_____.
- I weigh _____.
- I choose to eat only healthful foods because _____.

3. PERSONAL DEVELOPMENT: KNOWLEDGE, EDUCATION, SELF-IMPROVEMENT

"Happy is a man who finds wisdom and who acquires understanding." (Prov. 3:13)

"Get wisdom, get understanding; don't forget or turn away from the words of my mouth. Don't abandon wisdom, and she will watch over you; love her, and she will guard you. Wisdom is supreme—so get wisdom. And whatever else you get, get understanding."
(Prov. 4:5–7)

"Never rest on your achievements; always nurture your potential."—Denis Waitley

Beginning Today!	*One-Year Goals*	*Five-Year Goals*

Your success, financial and otherwise, will never far exceed your personal development.

Peter Drucker says that knowledge by definition makes itself obsolete. The only thing that will allow you to be a leader in today's environment is to be a continuous learner. Don't end your education when you finish high school, college, etc. Why do you think they call it *commencement*?

"Know thyself and to thine own self be true."
—Shakespeare

"The unexamined life is not worth living."
—Socrates

- Henry Ward Beecher called the first hour of the day the "rudder of the day."
- Read to set yourself apart from the rest of the world.
- Don't make excuses for lack of degrees; "educate" yourself.
- Remember the simple lessons of life: "All I really need to know I learned in kindergarten."

What is one thing you've put off because of the risk of failure? _____

_____

_____

_____

If you were to learn a new language, what would it be? Do you have the desire to do this?

_____

_____

_____

How many books will you read this year? Studies show that if you read 3 books on any subject you will be an expert in that topic. And if you read for 10 minutes each day, you will read about 1 average book per month. Twelve books could transform your life.

What are 3 or 4 books you'd like to read? _____

_____

_____

_____

Take the time for personal development, which is the inhaling part of healthy personal breathing. If you do nothing but exhale, you'll turn blue and pass out.

(Speaking of time, join the Automobile University. If you drive twenty-five thousand miles a year at an average speed of forty-six miles per hour, you will spend about the same amount of time in your car as an average college student spends in the classroom. The question then is, what are you doing with that time? You can listen to audio CDs and transform your success.)

How much time do you spend in your car each month? What could you do if you used that time wisely? _____

_____

_____

_____

Where do you look for inspiration, mentors, and positive input? _____

_____

_____

_____

What gifts do you have that you have not been using? Is there some potential for full achievement that needs to be unlocked? _____

_____

_____

_____

4. FAMILY: RELATIONSHIP TO OTHERS, DEVELOPMENT OF CHILDREN, IDEAL LOCATION TO LIVE

Each of these seven areas requires consistent, planned deposits for success to occur. Success in relationships doesn't occur just by default any more than just showing up makes you a success at work.

The second law of thermodynamics is things left to themselves tend to deteriorate. Great relationships don't just happen; they come as the result of making deposits toward the success you want.

Beginning Today!	*One-Year Goals*	*Five-Year Goals*

Here's the family mission statement we adopted when our children were young. We measured each activity in our household by this guide.

A Safe Place

"In a safe place people are kind. Sarcasm, fighting, backbiting and name-calling are exceptions. Kindness, consideration and forgiveness are the way of life. In a safe place there is laughter. Not just the canned laughter of television, but real laughter that comes from sharing meaningful work and play. In a safe place there are rules. The rules are few and fair and are made by the people who live and work there, including the children. In a safe place people listen to one another. They care about one another and show that they do. Please God, make this a Safe Place."—Mary MacCraken

Family is the smallest form of government. The current challenges in our government are merely a reflection of the breakdown of the American family. We start with the family and work up, not the other way around.

"Whatever the era, whatever the times, one thing will never change: fathers and mothers, if you have children, they must come first. You must read to your children and you must hug your children and you must love your children. Your success as a family, our success as a society, depends not on what happens in the

White House, but on what happens inside your house."—Barbara
Bush, reported in *The Washington Post*, June 2, 1990, 2 (from a
speech to graduates of Wellesley College)

What is the kind and length of vacation you will take this year? What is your goal for free time with family and friends? _____

_____

_____

_____

How could you substitute time you normally spend watching a favorite television show to spend that time instead with your spouse, a child, or a friend?_____

_____

_____

_____

Don't say you want to be a *better* mom, dad, or parent. Define what that means: You may decide to spend 20 minutes each night with your child or 1 Saturday morning a month doing what the child wants to do. Or how about scheduling 1 overnight event with your spouse every quarter?

What can you do starting today to be more successful is this area? _____

_____

_____

_____

5. SPIRITUAL: SPIRITUAL GROWTH, PERSONAL COMMITMENT, THEOLOGICAL UNDERSTANDING

"Search me, God, and know my heart; test me and know my
concerns. See if there is any offensive way in me; lead me in the
everlasting way." (Ps. 139:23–24)

| *Beginning Today!* | *One-Year Goals* | *Five-Year Goals* |

Can you say that you are now living out God's purpose for your life?_____

_____

_____

_____

What are you a part of that goes beyond yourself? _____

_____

_____

_____

How have you handled a crisis this last year? _____

_____

_____

_____

Are you comfortable taking steps of faith that may lead you in new directions, or are you more comfortable with maintaining what you've already seen?_____

_____

_____

_____

Do you trust your dreams as being inspired? _____

_____

_____

_____

Do your actions show connection and involvement with your faith community and your neighborhood? _____

_____

_____

_____

How would you like to be remembered?_____

_____

_____

_____

6. SOCIAL: INCREASED NUMBER OF FRIENDS, COMMUNITY INVOLVEMENT, ETC.

"The greatest good you can do for another is not just to share your riches, but to reveal to him his own."—Benjamin Disraeli

Change old attitudes. Discard past negatives. Ask for forgiveness. Make things right with people whom you need to forgive or who need to forgive you.

Beginning Today!	*One-Year Goals*	*Five-Year Goals*

Whom do you need to ask for forgiveness? _____

_____

_____

_____

Choose someone you could care for or be a mentor to, and then make the effort to work on this relationship starting today.

For whom could you show genuine concern? _____

_____

_____

_____

For whom could you be a mentor? _____

_____

_____

_____

What is a promise you made to someone but failed to keep? _____

_____

_____

_____

If you could spend time with an elderly person and find out some of his/her fondest memories, who would that person be? _____

_____

_____

_____

What regular, practical ways do you receive friendship, encouragement, and accountability from your current friends? _____

_____

_____

_____

Here is a system of useful principles from the classic book *How to Win Friends and Influence People* by Dale Carnegie.

Six Ways to Make People Like You
   1. Become genuinely interested in other people.
   2. Smile.
   3. Remember that a person's name is to that person the sweetest and most important sound in any language.
   4. Be a good listener. Encourage others to talk about themselves.
   5. Talk in terms of the other person's interests.
   6. Make the other person feel important—and do it sincerely.
   Practice these today to increase your social success.

7. CAREER: AMBITIONS, DREAMS, HOPES, INCOME GENERATION

"It is also the gift of God whenever anyone eats, drinks, and
enjoys all his efforts." (Eccles. 3:13)

"To work is to pray."—St. Augustine

"Opportunity lies in the man, not in the job."

| *Beginning Today!* | *One-Year Goals* | *Five-Year Goals* |

Career success is an outcome of knowing what success in the other 6 areas looks like. Your career should be a reflection of the life you want. Once you decide on the life you want, it becomes obvious what kind of work embraces that. Then you can truly plan your work around the life you want.

What are your unique (1) skills and abilities, (2) personality traits, and (3) values, dreams, and passions. These will define your best applications for work.

What is something you know you have the ability to do but you are confident it's not your calling or purpose in life? _____

_____

_____

_____

Describe how your current work contributes to your sense of personal mission and ideal work?

_____

_____

_____

How much of your sense of worth, identity, and status comes from your work? _____

_____

_____

_____

What would be the effect of losing this tomorrow? (Or what has been the effect of losing this?)

_____

_____

_____

How do you see your calling or passion connecting with your daily work? _____

_____

_____

_____

Do you feel your strongest gifts are used in your work?_____

_____

_____

_____

Do you feel your strongest gifts are used at home? _____

_____

_____

Do you feel your strongest gifts are used in your church? _____

_____

_____

_____

Do you feel your strongest gifts are used in your community? _____

_____

_____

_____

How would you describe the season of life in which you are now? _____

_____

_____

_____

Where are the main imbalances in your life that you would like to address? _____

_____

_____

_____

Congratulations! You have just put yourself into a 3 percent category of people. Having clear goals is the first step toward achieving extraordinary success in your life.

TAKEAWAYS

1. We tend to drift through life. Taking the path of least resistance makes crooked rivers and frustrated people.
2. Goals do not restrict us; they release us in a focused direction.
3. The best way to predict your future is to create it.
4. We tend to end up where we expect to end up. "For as he thinks within himself, so he is" (Prov. 23:7).

REFLECTIONS ON WORK MATERIAL

1. Review chapter 3.
2. Isn't it a natural tendency to plan our life around our work? Is work really the center of our lives?
3. Review the life balance material in chapter 4. Expect to define success in 7 areas rather than in just career or finances. Make sure you understand the necessity of being specific in your goals.
4. Everyone has dreams. "I want a bigger house, more money, to travel, etc." Those are just that—dreams. A dream becomes a goal by having a time frame. So if you say, "I want a 3,200 square feet house by June of next year and I will commit $500 extra a month toward

the down payment until then." Now we have a goal. It's specific and measurable. Make sure the goals are that specific. Review the process in chapter 4.

Assignments for Next Section

1. Clarify (1) skills and abilities, (2) personality traits, and (3) values, dreams, and passions.
2. Begin to consider work applications that blend all 3.
3. Listen to the second half of CD 1.

Section III

Planning My Work around the Life I Want!

1. The more we know about ourselves, the more confidence we can have about proper direction.
2. Steven Covey, author of *Seven Habits of Highly Effective People*, says the only way we can handle change is to know what is changeless about us.
3. The personality inventory categories are based on material that goes all the way back to Hippocrates. He understood that we are pretty predictable. This is an important section for integration into the work you do. The personality section looks at behavior, not ability.

Chapter Five

Looking Inward

Looking inward first is the only realistic way to develop a proper direction outward. I tell people that 85 percent of the process of having the confidence of proper direction is to look inward. Fifteen percent is the application—résumés, job search, interviewing, starting your own business, etc. Our society teaches us to put the cart before the horse—to get a job and then make your life work. Wrong! To have real "success" you must understand yourself and plan your life first, then plan your work to embrace the life you want.

Experts estimate that as many as 70 percent of American workers are unhappy with their jobs. It would be ludicrous to think that there are that many bad jobs or that many bad people. The problem is that those people have not first taken the time to look at themselves before getting those jobs. The time spent looking at yourself will provide a 100 percent payback in terms of helping you create a proper direction. The more you know about yourself, the more confidence you can have about choosing the right work environment.

In what kind of settings are you most comfortable? _____

_____

_____

_____

_____

How do you respond to management? _____

_____

_____

_____

How would you manage other people? _____

_____

_____

_____

_____

Are you better working with people, things, or ideas? _____

_____

_____

_____

Are you more analytical, detailed, and logical, or are you one to see the big picture and respond with emotion and enthusiasm? _____

_____

_____

_____

Are you steady and predictable, or do you seek variety and new challenges? _____

_____

_____

_____

Are you verbal and persuasive, or are you a caring, empathetic listener?_____

_____

_____

_____

These questions will assist you in defining the kind of work you for which you are most suited.

Any job you have must blend three personal areas. These areas will be developed as you work through the material.

1. Skills and Abilities

Yes, you must have the ability to do your job, but keep in mind that skill or ability alone will not necessarily lead to a sense of purpose, fulfillment, and meaningful accomplishment. You may have the ability to make perfect wooden wheels, but there may be little redeeming value in doing so. At the same time you may be an excellent dentist and yet be unfulfilled in doing dentistry. Many people have demonstrated the ability to do something well and yet are miserable in doing it day after day.

I have worked with many attorneys who have proven their ability to do the work, but they are miserable in their day-to-day activities. The same can be said for many physicians, pastors, plumbers, and painters. Having great eyesight is not enough reason for you to be an airline pilot. Having good hand coordination could be a component of being a great assembly line worker or a brain surgeon but in and of itself is not enough reason to pursue either. Having a grasp of accounting principles could make you a CPA or a professional gambler, but you can see the fallacy in having that ability alone direct your path.

What strengths or abilities have others who know you well noticed in you? _____

_____

_____

_____

2. Personality Tendencies

How do you relate to other people? In what kinds of environments are you most comfortable? Are you a people person, or are you more comfortable with projects and tasks? Are you expressive and visionary, or are you analytical, logical, and detailed? Do you like a predictable environment, or do you seek change, challenge, and variety? Clarification here will help you identify the best working situation for yourself (more on this in the next few pages).

List five words or phrases that describe you. _____

_____

_____

_____

3. Values, Dreams, and Passions

What is it that you find naturally enjoyable? If money were not important, what would you spend your time doing? When do you find the time just flying by? What are those recurring themes that keep coming up in your thinking? What did you enjoy as a child but perhaps have been told was unrealistic or impractical to focus on as a career? _____

_____

_____

_____

This is a tough area for most people I work with. There is a subtle spiritual myth that following our dreams is selfish, egotistical, and something God would frown on. However, we are created in God's image and as such are creators ourselves. Why would God have created us to think imaginatively and to have vivid dreams only to squelch those dreams for practicality? I encourage you to trust your dreams as having come from a divine source. And as you move toward your values, dreams, and passions, you will, in fact, move toward being more spiritual and more fully what God created you to be.

I find many people have squandered their own creative energies by investing largely in the hopes, dreams, plans, and expectations of others. Well-meaning parents, friends, teachers, and pastors may have exerted subtle control to obscure and misdirect your own directions. I frequently find professionals in their 40s and 50s

> "To live a creative life, we must lose our fear of being wrong."
> —Joseph Chilton Pearce

who are discovering that the life they are living is not their own. Wanting encouragement and support is natural, and we seek this first from our nuclear family, then from an ever-widening circle of friends and people of influence. Unfortunately, this encouragement seldom supports a really individualized path, but rather the broad applications of "doctor, dentist, teacher, lawyer, plumber, engineer," etc. Caution is the common response to anything radically different or unique in application. Thus, adding parental and others' fear to their own, the "safe" path is chosen. And there, caught between exciting dreams and the fear of failure, boring career paths are born.

Thus, the most frequently stated challenge I hear is, "I'm still trying to figure out what I want to be when I grow up." This is often said as an embarrassing self-revelation from a 45-year old. You must realize this is a healthy and realistic starting point. It's very difficult to see all the options clearly and have the necessary self-understanding at 18 to be able to ask the right questions, much less to be able to make the right choices. Creating proper life direction is an ongoing process, and yes, it can be intimidating and exhilarating at the same time. Value the life experience you have had. Even if unfulfilling and misdirected, it will help provide the clarity by which you can now make really good decisions.

The fulfilling path is usually one to be discovered right under a person's nose. Normally there have been recurring themes in one's life—moments of recognizing being "connected" or "in the zone." In the movie *Chariots of Fire*, Eric Liddle was told by his sister to forget his passion for running and return to the worthy family missionary ministry. A line from that movie still gives me goose bumps when I hear it. Eric says: "God made me fast, and when I run I feel his pleasure." Don't think this is a time to ignore your true passions even if the normal applications do not seem to produce the income results. A little time spent looking at yourself will provide a big payback in terms of selecting and structuring an opportunity around your unique strengths.

> *"To know what you prefer instead of humbly saying 'Amen' to what the world tells you you ought to prefer, is to have kept your soul alive."*
> —*Robert Louis Stevenson*

If you received a 3 million-dollar inheritance today, what would you do? How would your life change? _____

_____

_____

_____

Think back over the dreams you had as a child. How does your present position in life compare to that? _____

_____

_____

_____

Be thinking and writing notes in these three areas.

The integration will be critical and will lead you to recognize clear and consistent patterns, identifying areas of opportunity for career application. Look for the unusual application of your uniqueness. If I say "schoolteacher," the first thing that comes to mind may be a metro school classroom with 32.5 kids in the classroom; however, you could be a teacher working for IBM, living in London, England. All you need is one unique

> *"God has given each of you some special abilities; be sure to use them to help each other, passing on to others God's many kinds of blessings." (1 Pet. 4:10 TLB)*

application of what integrates these three components for you. This is an individualized process. There is no cookie-cutter plan for everyone, even if there are similarities in background, age, and education.

"When written in Chinese, the word 'crisis' is composed of
two characters—one represents danger, and the other
represents opportunity."—John F. Kennedy

We hear a lot today about leaving a legacy. In writing your epitaph, what would you want people to remember about you? _____

_____

_____

_____

_____

_____

_____

Work through the simple inventories provided in the next chapter to help in clarifying general categories. This is not to put you in a box but to help use your strengths.

"Those who loved you and were helped by you will remember you. So carve your name on hearts and not on marble."
—C. H. Spurgeon

RISK—DANGER OR OPPORTUNITY?

I frequently hear people say they would not want to try a new job, a new sport, a new car, or a different route to the office because of the "risk" involved. Certainly, we hear this especially when a person is considering a new career or changing positions. Why leave the predictable for the unpredictable? And yet, that may be the core of the issue here. If you go to Las Vegas and put the deed to your house down on a roll of the dice, that's gambling—risking with no reasonable control or plan. However, if you are in a negative work environment and you have checked out your options and are moving to a solid organization with a higher income, how can that be called "risk"? Risk implies jumping off a cliff with no idea what is at the bottom. In business or career moves, we greatly reduce risk by having a careful plan of action. Call it "seizing an opportunity" rather than "risk." Sometimes the greatest risk is not taking one.

Chapter Six

Understanding My Personal Characteristics

As already stated, the first 85 percent of creating a proper direction is to look inward. Here you will have the opportunity to look more specifically at your personality traits, knowing that you want to embrace those in a proper work fit.

Instructions: In each box, circle each word or phrase that describes a consistent character trait of yours. You should find groupings in one or two categories. Then turn to the next page for the personal style overview.

Dominance (Driver)	Influencing (Expressive)	Compliance (Analytical)	Steadiness (Amiable)
Likes Authority	Enthusiastic	Perfectionist	Calm
Takes Charge	Spontaneous	Controlled	Loyal
Controlling	Enjoys Change	Predictable	Nurturing
Bold	Group Oriented	Inquisitive	Sympathetic
Decision Maker	Likes Variety	Accurate	Conscientious
Overlooks Details	Creates New Ideas	Orderly	Peacemaker
Not Careful of Other's Feelings	Optimistic	Factual	Enjoys Routine
Adventurous	Infectious Laughter	Reserved	Good Listener
Determined	Inspirational	Scheduled	Reliable
Self-Reliant	Promoter	Courteous	Relaxed
Independent	Can Waste Time	Conventional	Understanding
Confident	Entertains Others	Restrained	Friendly
Very Direct	Initiator	Methodical	Stable
Competitive	Stimulating	High Standards	Avoids Conflict
Takes Risks	Negotiates Conflict	Mature	Passive
Challenges the Status Quo	Trusting	Exacting	Deliberate
		Evasive	Sincere
			Possessive

Daring	Convincing	Patient	Steady
Impatient	Persuasive	Logical	Caring
Demanding	Charming	Detailed	
Results Oriented	Talkative		

This is an abbreviated personal style overview. We can produce a thorough 35-page fully personalized career planning report for you by simple setting up an Internet link and password. You will be able to complete the survey and receive your full report immediately, including a list of suggested careers based on your personal style responses. Our normal price is $75, but your discounted option is provided for only $37.50. You can purchase this directly from our products page at http://www.48days.com/index.php#career_report. See full sample report before your purchase.

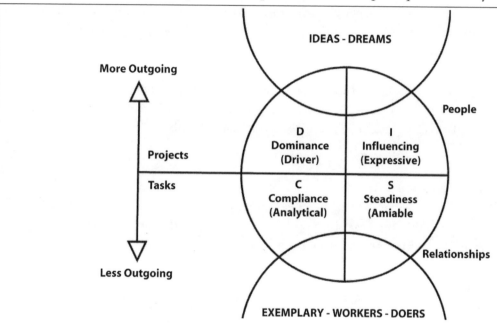

18% D	28% I	40% S	14% C
"Let's do it now!"	"Trust me! It'll work out!"	"Let's keep things the way they are!"	"How was it done in the past?"
Strengths	**Strengths**	**Strengths**	**Strengths**
Takes charge	Good talkers	Steady	Loves detail
Likes power & authority	Outgoing	Loyal	Very logical
Confident - Very direct	Entertains others	Good listeners	Diplomatic
Adventurous, Bold	Fun loving	Calm	Factual
Determined	Impulsive	Enjoys routine	Deliberate
Competitive	Enjoys change	Sympathetic	Controlled
Self-reliant	Creative	Patient	Inquisitive
	Energetic	Understanding	Predictable
	Optimistic	Reliable	
	Promoter		
Weaknesses	**Weaknesses**	**Weaknesses**	**Weaknesses**
Can hurt others' feelings	Can waste time	Avoids conflict	Can appear rigid
Can turn people off	Won't be quiet and listen	Can be slow to act	Resistant to change
Overlooks details	Loses sight of the task	Maintains a low profile	Too serious
		May seem unrealistic	

% of people in the general population high in this category

Personal Style Overview

Please be assured that there are no right or wrong characteristics here. There tends to be in all of us a little of the "grass is greener on the other side of the fence." It's easy to wish we were more like someone else—quicker to speak up or more outgoing or better with details, etc. The goal in all of this is not to have an even amount of each category but to see extreme highs in 1 or 2 of the 4 categories. You will be most effective and fulfilled by confirming those 1 or 2 areas and then finding work that embraces those characteristics.

Ranking these categories will help you see strong messages that one person is opinionated, another is encouraging and nurturing, 1 is good with things and details, while the next is expressive and has to be around people. There is no good or bad, right or wrong about any of this. They are just differences, but the more we recognize the consistent trends, the more we can see the application in work.

Talk through the four areas with people who know you well, describing both the positive and the negative signs. Giving animal names to the 4 categories will help in recognizing them in yourself and in people you meet daily.

- Dominance (D): Lion—Bold, daring, goes where no one else will go
- Influencing (I): Otter—always flitting around, socializing with others
- Steadiness (S): Golden Retriever—faithful, loyal, nonjudgmental
- Compliance (C): Beaver—puts nose the task, great with details

Or Bird Names
- Dominance (D): Eagle—rise above, can go alone
- Influencing (I): Peacock—watch me, the cheerleaders
- Steadiness (S): Dove—the universal bird for peace, loving, and kind
- Compliance (C): Owl—may not say much but doesn't miss a thing

Or Biblical Characters
- Dominance (D): Apostle Paul—Bold, opinionated. Every time he got around someone else in a position of authority, there was conflict. Virtually everyone who went out on road trips with him came back home with their feelings hurt. And yet Paul gave us 13 books of the New Testament and more teaching about how to build churches and how to live the Christian life than anyone else.
- Influencing (I): Peter—Quick to speak his mind, and it frequently got him in trouble. But he was the trusted friend and follower of Jesus.
- Steadiness (S): Moses—Not a pushy, up-front leader. But he was loyal; for forty years he led those complaining, whiny people. Even when God lost his patience and wanted to wipe the people out, Moses said, "No, let's give them another chance." Always compassionate.
- Compliance (C): Luke—Gathered lots of facts before reporting something as true. He was a scientist, a physician by vocation.

Now look at the following career applications. Be careful of wanting to find your specific career application here. This is a short, nonexhaustive list intended only to show the grouping of careers and how they embrace similar careers. But with so many options and the wealth of nontraditional jobs today, the perfect one may not be here. It may need to be created.

DOMINANCE	INFLUENCING	STEADINESS	COMPLIANCE
Manufacturer's	Training	Investigator	Medical Record
Representative	Representative	Pharmacist	Technician
Lobbyist	Clergy Member	Licensed Practical	Procurement Clerk
Business Manager	Advertising Manager	Nurse	Secretary
Travel Guide	Real Estate Appraiser	Optometrist	Accountant
Principal	Newspaper Editor	Truck Driver	Job Analyst
Dancer	Outside Sales Agent	Counselor	Mail Clerk
Fashion Coordinator	Business	Social Worker	Caseworker
Landscape Architect	Administrator	Teacher,	Architect
Real Estate	Home Economist	Secondary School	Pathologist
Sales Agent	Actor/Actress	Market Research	Biochemist
Production	Reporter	Analyst	Actuary
Coordinator	Illustrator	Veterinarian	Audio Visual
Show	Faculty Member	Nurse, General Duty	Production Specialist
Host/Hostess	Interior Designer	Administrator	Dentist
Manager,	Arbitrator	Programmer	Geologist
Customer Services	Artist	Lab Technician	Furniture Designer
Announcer	Sales Manager	Correction Officer	Physician's Assistant
Writer	Event Coordinator	Horticulturist	Historian
Entrepreneur	Graphic Designer	Chiropractor	Environmental
Business Owner	Public Speaker	Librarian	Analyst
Automobile Sales Agent	Politician	Claim Adjuster	Airline Pilot Drafting
CEO		Factory Worker	Designer
Inventor			
Interpreter			

OCCUPATIONAL CATEGORIES

In the box above are some of the occupations that line up with the personal characteristics you checked on the previous pages. These are broad categories but will give you an idea of what occupations would be most fitting for you. This is not a complete list but will give you an idea of how different jobs use the same personal skills.

Don't think you have to find your perfect job in this short list; however, you should be able to see how personal skills are naturally used in certain job categories. Recognize the thousands of possibilities. You may be high in the S and C categories and be a great candidate for an accounting position where you stay with the same company for 25 years. But those same characteristics could make you a great candidate for a totally entrepreneurial self-owned business where you sell gardening tools and gadgets on the Internet, never having face-to-face contact with your customers but making $150,000 a year. Don't limit the possibilities too quickly from any list. The possibilities are endless, and you have the potential and the ability to create the perfect work.

TAKEAWAYS

1. I am unique. I am fearfully and wonderfully made.
2. There is no right or wrong, good or bad here. There is only the opportunity to match your uniqueness with the right career choice. Every job has personality. Will it match what you bring to the table?
3. God never buries our uniqueness. His perfect plan will enhance our true personality traits.

ASSIGNMENTS FOR NEXT SESSION

1. Review Résumé Myths.
2. Update your résumé.
3. Study the job search process. This is an important section.
4. Review interviewing in chapter 9. Begin to practice answering the questions likely to be asked in an Interview.
5. Listen to the first half of CD 2.

48 DAYS
Hall of Fame

At the age of 15, Melissa went to work for McDonalds. Fifteen years later, she had completed her college degree and had moved up in the McDonalds organization. However, she was convinced that loyalty had trapped her in the fast food industry. Her résumé confirmed that she was simply a faithful fast food worker.

In talking with Melissa, it became clear that the one thing she had most enjoyed in those 15 years, was working with the McKids program. This is a program where they bring mentally and physically challenged kids into the stores and help them with real world work experience. Melissa was guided in restructuring her résumé to highlight her competencies in working with disabilities and in creating a clear focus for her job search. In this ideal example, her first interview was with the state of Tennessee. She was hired as the head of a disabilities program, totally redirecting her career and moving her, in one day, from $18,000 to $38,000 in annual pay.

Nothing was added to what Melissa already had at her disposal. It was simply a process of changing how she was presenting herself and having a clear focus for the job search.

(See www.48Days.com.)

Section IV

Nuts and Bolts

1. The most important work is now completed and you are ready for the application or what we call the nuts and bolts. Having a clear personal understanding and focus is 85 percent of the process.
2. The résumé is to be a sales tool for where you are going. Usually a person's résumé is just a chronological review and history of where they've been. That may or may not be what you want.
3. The creative job search strategy is frequently the most powerful component to get people the results they want. We can find the 87 percent of the jobs that are never advertised in the newspapers.
4. *Interviewing* means "to see about each other." Most hiring decisions are made in the first 3 to 5 minutes of an interview. We know what is being evaluated in those first critical minutes.

Chapter Seven

Shaping the Options

Now that you have looked at yourself, you are ready to begin to look outward at the best options. Only after you have a clear sense of what is unique about you can we start to talk about the applications that fit you. It doesn't matter that there are many opportunities in health care, telecommunications, computer technology or that the hottest selling franchise is Papa John's Pizza. These only have relevance after you know your:

1. skills and abilities,
2. personality traits,
3. values, dreams, and passions

Résumés, Job Search Strategies, and Interviewing

Résumés, job searches, interviewing, and negotiating salaries comprise the logistical part of finding the traditional work you love. Now that you have laid the proper foundation, we can look at these important details. Many people see the résumé as the most important part of the hiring process, believing that companies make hiring decisions from them. A company would be foolish to make a hiring decision from a résumé. You don't want your résumé to tell the company enough about you so that it could make an intelligent decision about hiring you. All you want it to do is wet the interviewer's appetite enough so that he or she wants to see you personally. In the interview the rubber meets the road. Everything else is preliminary.

Your résumé is your sales tool for where you want to go. Don't let it be just a snapshot of where you have been. That may or may not be advantageous for you. Recently, I was working with a woman who had from all appearances had a successful career in accounting. She had consistently moved up in positions and was in a prestigious managerial role with a worldwide bank. In that position she was responsible for daily transactions of millions of dollars. Guess what she hated more than anything? Yes, accounting and financial management. In her own description she had built her career around an ability having no connection with her personality or passions. Her résumé reflected her long, illustrious career in accounting. But why would we present her and position her in a way designed to duplicate those duties? We restructured her résumé to show areas of competence like training, supervising, planning, and operations. These were proven abilities of hers and allowed her to present herself as a candidate for something with a different day-to-day focus and much more suited to her personality style.

If you want to redirect your career path, you can begin the process with a well-designed résumé. If your résumé is just a chronological history of what you've done, it will pigeonhole you into continuing to do what you've always done. You can redirect in major ways by identifying "areas of competence" that would have application in new companies, industries, and professions. Make sure your résumé is a sales tool for where you want to go, not just a chronological snapshot of where you have been.

Knowing how to conduct your job search process will transform the results you can expect. Many people become convinced that they are not pretty enough, do not have the right degrees, are too old, too young, or are getting a bad reference from a former employer. How you conduct the job search process will have far more to do with your success than any of those factors.

We are also going to look at how to find the "hidden" job opportunities. We know that only about 12 percent of jobs ever appear in the newspaper, on the Internet, or in another form of advertising. You can find those unadvertised positions and drastically reduce the competition you face for them.

Even though we know that the average job is now only 3.2 years in length, most people remain unprepared for the interview process. They believe that they can send out the résumé, have some company decide it has to have them, and simply show up for a routine interview. Few things could be further from the truth.

The interview is the critical part of this whole process. This is where you have the opportunity to sell yourself and negotiate the most desirable position. Time spent in preparation and practice will be a great investment of your time.

Knowing that most hiring decisions are made in the first 3 to 5 minutes of an interview confirms that the interviewer is not looking at the fine print on the fourth page of your résumé, but rather is asking him/herself:

- Do I like this person?
- Will Frank fit in well with the team?
- Is Joan honest?
- Is Dave fun to be around?

These questions are probably going through the interviewer's mind in those first few critical seconds. Be careful of resting on your academic credentials and work experience. Today, more than ever, companies realize that they hire a whole person, not just a set of definable skills. Remember, you are there to *sell* yourself as the best candidate.

REAL PREDICTORS OF SUCCESS

With all the options and opportunities for jobs, what are the real predictors of success? Isn't *ability* still the best predictor of success?

The 5 predictors of success are:

1. Passion: A person with passion is a person who can set goals. Without them, you can have no clear direction and will drift along the road of circumstances.

Position yourself on this scale for passion:

Lethargic...Passionate

2. Determination: Without a clear purpose, any obstacle will send a person in a new direction. Without determination you will easily be lured away from your path.

Position yourself on this scale for determination:

Unsure..Determined

3. Talent: No one has talent in every area, but everyone has talent. Discover where you rise to the top. What are those things you love to do whether or not you get paid?

Position yourself on this scale for talent:

Jack-of-All-Trades..Focused Talent

4. Self-discipline: Without self-discipline, a person can easily be swayed by others. Self-discipline is the foundation that makes the others work.

Position yourself on this scale for self-discipline:

Easily Swayed..Self-Disciplined

5. Faith: Even with everything lining up logically, there still comes that step of faith into the unknown. You cannot reach new lands if you keep one foot on the shore.

Position yourself on this scale for faith:

Lacking Belief...Strong Faith

RÉSUMÉ MYTHS

Consider the following myths:

Myth 1: A good résumé and cover letter will get me the job.

Résumés and letters do not get jobs; they advertise for interviews. A résumé should not tell enough to make a hiring decision. It should simply entice the reader to want to see you.

Myth 2: The candidate with the best education, skills, and experience will always get the position.

Many factors are considered in a hiring decision. Education, skills, age, and ability are only a few of the hiring criteria. Employers interview because they want to see you—how you look, interact, and fit in with their organization.

A recent Yale University study reported that 15 percent of the reason for a person's success is due to technical skill and knowledge, and 85 percent of the reason originates from that person's personal skill: attitude, enthusiasm, self-discipline, desire, and ambition.

This is why candidates with the best qualifications on paper frequently do not get the job.

Myth 3: You can plan all you want, but getting a job is really a matter of luck, who you know, or being in the right place at the right time.

Luck is what happens to people who have clear goals and detailed plans of action. Don't deceive yourself by buying into the luck myth. As with everything valuable in life, getting a great position comes as a result of having a clear plan.

Myth 4: Employers appreciate long résumés because more information saves time spent interviewing.

Most résumés get a 30- to 40-second look. You must be able to communicate clearly in that time your areas of competence. There is seldom a reason to go beyond 2 pages in length.

Myth 5: Always put your salary requirements on your résumé.

This can only work against you. Whether high or low, it has no positive purpose on a résumé. Salary is to be negotiated after the employer decides you are the right person for the job. Only when an employer wants you and you want them is it appropriate to discuss compensation. Anything prior to that will work against you.

Myth 6: You should always close a cover letter with, "I look forward to hearing from you."

Never! Even in times of low unemployment, expecting the receiver to take the initiative is unrealistic. Remember, you must always take the initiative. State when you will call to follow up: "I will call you Thursday morning concerning any questions we both may have and to discuss a personal meeting."

This may appear to be pushy or assertive, and it may be. But what you want is action! Persistence pays.

Myth 7: The more résumés you send, the more you increase your chances of getting a job.

Not necessarily. 30 to 40 résumés combined with quality introduction letters, cover letters, and follow-up phone calls are much more effective than 1,000 résumés sent out alone.

Myth 8: Once you send your résumé, all you can do is wait.

If you take no action, you will likely get no results. Always follow up by phone.

"You can do anything if you have enthusiasm. Enthusiasm is the yeast that makes your hopes rise to the stars. Enthusiasm is the spark in your eye, the swing in your gait, the grip of your hand, the irresistible surge of your will and your energy to execute your ideas. Enthusiasts are fighters, they have fortitude, they have staying qualities. Enthusiasm is at the bottom of all progress! With it, there is accomplishment. Without it, there are only alibis."—Henry Ford

The major quest in life is not what you are *getting*, but what you are *becoming*.

DESIGNING A RÉSUMÉ

TRANSFERABLE SKILLS AND ABILITIES

This section deals with building your résumé so it does become a sales tool for getting you the position you want. You can present yourself as a top candidate for sales and marketing, administration, organization, developing, training—or whatever your dream position is—if you draw from your experience and identify it in an advantageous way.

1. Your transferable skills are the most basic unit of whatever career you choose. Skills serve as a bridge from one job to another. Once you have mastered a skill in one career, you can transfer that skill to another field and to another career. These skills can also be rearranged, if desired, in a way that opens up a new and different career.

2. You always want to claim the highest skills possible. The résumé is the place to brag on yourself; don't be modest. This does not always mean to focus on your highest degrees. There are many times when an advanced degree actually misdirects a person from their desired goal. Just remember to highlight what you want to be noticed and embraced in your next position.

3. Be specific. If you are dependable, reliable, doing what is expected of you, and showing up for work on time, you can get any entry-level job today. But as good as they are, those characteristics do little to separate you from everyone else out there. The more specific you can be about what makes you unique, the fewer the competitors and the more you can move up the financial ladder. At 35 or 45 years old, a person has much more to emphasize than they could have at 25, even with the same degrees behind them. If you are 25 you can highlight things you did as a volunteer in your school, community, or church, in addition to competencies used in paid positions.

4. The higher your transferable skills, the less competition you will face for whatever job you are seeking. Keep in mind that jobs using higher skills are more challenging to find because they are rarely advertised through traditional methods.

5. There is not one right format for creating a résumé. If you have had increasing levels of responsibility and want to continue in that industry, a straight chronological format may be the best one for you. If you want to redirect your career, then a more functional format will help you. A combination of both chronological and functional is common and can work well for most people today.

6. You should cover at least 10 years in your work experience—longer if there is some specific experience that strengthens your presentation. Don't worry if you are just starting into the workforce; draw from areas of competence that you have proven in your school, church, or community.

7. Having multiple jobs is no longer the red flag it once was. Companies realize that to advance, you may have to move on. They also realize that in today's volatile workplace, good people are frequently let go through no fault of their own. But you don't have to list every position that you held for a short time. Also, feel free to list only years rather than months on your résumé to draw attention away from the short length of some positions.

Recognizing that your résumé is your sales brochure, how effective do you think your résumé is?

_____

_____

_____

You purchase clothing, furniture, cars, and candy bars based on the sales information you see about them. Does your sales information excite you? If you were a prospective buyer (employer), would you want to see more? _____

_____

_____

_____

Does the image created by your résumé distinctively set you apart from anyone else on the planet? Does it highlight your uniqueness based on your personal life experiences at this stage of your life? _____

_____

_____

_____

A CREATIVE, ACTIVE JOB SEARCH STRATEGY

Use the list on the next page as a stimulus to your thinking about your own transferable skills. Choose 8 to 10, and then try to narrow the list to 3 primary skills on which you want to focus. You are better off focusing on these skills than appearing to be a generalist. Identify what you do best and that you want to continue to do.

Circle the skill areas below that describe your highest areas of competence. Add to the list if you think of other words that describe areas of competence.

Assembling	Production
Maintenance	Repairing
Sculpting	Crafting
Construction	Expediting
Controlling	Operations
Managing	Supervising
Hiring	Communications
Instructing	Assessing
Evaluating	Motivating
Advising	Coaching
Empowering	Persuading
Presenting	Coordinating
Planning	Leading
Negotiating	Research
Organizing	Administration
Problem Solving	Systematizing
Programming	Filing
Computer Skills	Clerical Work
Training	Purchasing
Customer Service	Driving
Sales	Marketing
Accounting	Designing
Writing	Directing
Teaching	Implementation
Counseling	Financial Management
Public Relations	Recruiting
Promotions	Team Building
Transcribing	Tutoring
Mentoring	Producing
Arranging	Editing

Over the next several pages are some examples of real résumés. You will see that there are different formats, depending on the purpose of each résumé. Remember, the résumé is only your selling tool in an attempt to get an interview.

Feel free to use as much from the examples as you want. You can copy phrases that apply to your situation, but do personalize your résumé for yourself. Everything in it should work for you. If a piece of information does not help position you as a candidate for what you want to do, don't emphasize or draw attention to it.

Is Job-Hopping Still A Liability?

Changing jobs early and often, job hopping, isn't the liability it once was, says Allen Salikof, president and CEO of Management Recruiters International, Inc. It might even be a plus. Traditionally employers who saw a job-hopping pattern on a résumé would pass on that candidate in favor of one with more staying power. But job-hopping isn't necessarily the kiss of death anymore, says Salikof. More and more we find employers actually favoring a candidate who has moved around. Some are even put off by candidates who have stayed too long in one job or one company where their skills, particularly technological skills, have not had to keep pace with the marketplace. "If the candidate's history shows consistent increases in salary and responsibility, job-hopping may tag him or her as a hot property." In some industries you may have to explain why you stayed around so long. Talk about a reversal in traditional thinking!

The old model was to move up vertically in one company for career progress. That may have worked well in production environments, but it does not work well in our current knowledge-based work settings. In a knowledge-based environment, you will be much better off staying true to your strongest areas of competence and moving from company to company, using those same skills, for your career advancement. Thus we see the average job length of 3.2 years even for the most respected professionals.

EDUCATION—WHAT IS IT?

We continue to receive a barrage of e-mail containing concerns regarding education. "I'm 27, have a degree in psychology, and still don't know what I want to do." "My son has dropped out of college, and I'm concerned he's on a road to nowhere." "I'm an attorney, 4 years out of law school, and think I have made a mistake."

What is education? Is our traditional thinking about getting degrees still accurate? *Webster's* dictionary defines *education* as "the process of training and developing the knowledge, skill, mind, and character" of a person. With this definition we can readily see that education can occur in many ways and is certainly not confined to the traditional classroom.

I have spent much of my life involved in the academic world, having completed my bachelor's, master's, and doctoral studies. And yet I have been concerned about the overselling of that kind of education in our country. We know that 10 years after graduation, 80 percent of college graduates are working in something totally unrelated to their college degree. We see people that we consider successful like Bill Gates, Michael Dell, Maya Angelou, Donna Karan, Michelle Pfieffer, who are college dropouts. And most actors, performers, and business owners have not found college to be their key to success.

There are 2 reasons to go to school:

1. To get a piece of paper so someone will give you a job.
2. For the personal development that takes place.

If you go for the first reason only, you will probably be disappointed. The second can never be taken away. But recognize where personal development can take place. You may work on a construction crew, an organic farm, a day-care, or in a classroom. All are legitimate places for growth and education.

SAMPLE RÉSUMÉS

(Use a format like this if you want the focus to be on skills rather than on employment locations.) Notice the skills are described without being pigeonholed in any one industry. Company affiliations are de-emphasized. The focus is on areas of competence so that this candidate can change industries.

James Spencer
4598 Meadow Trace
Columbus, Ohio 44929
(419) 377-9845

SKILLS SUMMARY

Over 14 solid years of professional selling and sales management. Experienced in planning, organizing, and overseeing projects. Knowledgeable in hiring, training, and supervising. Team player in maintaining company policies and procedures. Committed to high work ethics and to attainment of management goals and objectives.

QUALIFICATIONS

ADMINISTRATION

Responsible for 21-person staff in current position. Increased gross revenues from $16.2M to $31.5M in 3-year period, while increasing pre-tax profit over 200 percent. Directed employee training and employee evaluations. Competent in dealing with compensation negotiation and conflict resolution. Able to handle variety of tasks and responsibilities simultaneously. Strong leadership skills and accountability to management. Provided valuable input for long-term planning and market assessment.

SALES

National Sales Manager of the Year. Closed largest commercial account in TN. Negotiated accounts with So. Central Bell and the new Columbus Arena. Closed first tier account program with 48 regional chain stores, involving in excess of $200K annually. Able to interact with key community and business leaders. Adept at recognizing customer needs and achieving balance between customer needs and company goals and policies. Personal commitment to integrity results in increased sales and customer confidence.

ORGANIZATIONAL SKILLS

Developed successful inside-marketing concept, which was given national rollout in 2001. Used TeleMagic software to establish pilot program, "Pricing for Profit," for 300 national offices. Designed palm-top computer usage for field representatives to streamline efficiency. Analyzed sales figures and business trends to increase sales.

PROFESSIONAL EXPERIENCE

BFI OF OHIO—COLUMBUS	—Columbus, OH	
Sales Manager	2001–Present	
WRIGHT INCORPORATED	—Worthington, OH	
Sales Manager	2000–2001	
ABC PRINTING, INC.	—Dayton, OH	
Sr. Account Manager	1994–2000	

ARC/AMS DIVISION OF
AMERICAN EXPRESS   —Columbus, OH
Sales Representative   1987–1994

EDUCATION
OHIO STATE UNIVERSITY
Columbus, Ohio 1983–1987

CLUBS AND ORGANIZATIONS
Who's Who Among Students in American Colleges
   and Universities
Big Brothers/Big Sisters—Board Member
Columbus Rotary Club
Columbus Chamber of Commerce

REFERENCES
Available upon request

This woman had only one employer, no college degree, and assumed she was trapped. But we emphasized transferable areas of competence, positioning her as a great candidate in other industries.

Joyce A. Parker
398 Manor View Lane
Brentwood, TN 37027
(615) 377-6798

SKILLS SUMMARY

Solid experience in multiple facets of office operations. Knowledgeable in data entry and computer functions. Proven skills in instructing and motivating coworkers. Committed to high work ethics and to attainment of management goals and objectives. Described by others as loyal, trustworthy, and fun-loving.

PROFESSIONAL EXPERIENCE

SOUTH CENTRAL BELL, Nashville, TN August 1983–Present

ORGANIZATION

Oversaw development and implementation of programs, switching from rural route numbers to house numbers. Increased efficiency of departmental system. Dealt with key community leaders to coordinate 911 system. Competent in technical areas with focus on detail and accuracy. Performed accounting functions including reconciling employee payroll records, data entry, and inventory management.

TRAINING

Confident in managing and supervising employees. Works well with all personality styles. Responsible for accuracy of incoming employee performance. Strong interpersonal skills with ability to diffuse workplace tension. Created departmental instruction manual. Coordinated employee hours and duties while building team spirit and commitment. Able to handle variety of tasks and responsibilities simultaneously. Strong accountability to management. Part of #1-rated office in 9-state region.

CUSTOMER SERVICE

Competent in setting up service and completing problem resolution. Assisted in negotiating customer concerns, leading to win-win solutions. Liaison between company and clients. Ability to communicate with customers in person or by telephone and to establish rapport and support.

EDUCATION

Nashville Technical Institute	—Beginning Electronic Telecommunications
Overton High School	—1983 Graduate

PROFESSIONAL SEMINARS

- *Be a People Pro*
- *Telecommunications Excellence*
- *Customer First Service*
- *The Quality Advantage*

REFERENCES

Available upon request

This writer has hands-on construction background but is moving into professional management.

Tom Phillips
187 Pepper Ridge Circle
Lakeland, Florida 23689
(863) 831-3587 .

SKILLS SUMMARY

Solid experience in management and supervision of construction field projects to completion. Possesses the skills to build, strengthen, and maintain people relationships. Excellent writing and verbal skills. Technical aptitude and background. Self-motivated in continuing education. Professional manner and personal commitment to high standards of integrity.

QUALIFICATIONS

MANAGEMENT

Accomplished in planning, scheduling, and directing construction projects to completion. On-site supervision of detailed homes valued up to $650,000. Assisted in planning for new upscale subdivision. Responsible for contractor-customer follow-up and liaison.

INTERPERSONAL SKILLS

Proven ability to interact positively with a wide range of people. Five years in field sales, selling premium-quality products and opening new accounts with follow-up, service, and repeat sales. Participated in field training of sales reps. Program included instructing, training, and evaluation with both trainees and home-office management. Won company-wide award for highest training sales production.

TECHNICAL ABILITY

Bachelor's degree in biology with chemistry minor. Resourceful in research and information searches. Self-taught in knowledge of selection and use of construction materials and structural requirements. Successful experience in understanding and operating within technical boundaries, focusing on detail and accuracy.

PROFESSIONAL EXPERIENCE

MAINTENANCE ENGINEERING—LAKELAND, FL
Sr. Field Trainer and Field Sales   May 1997–Present

ADEX CORPORATION—LAKELAND, FL
Superintendent of Construction   Jan. 1991–Nov. 1997

PRESERVATION CONSTRUCTION COMPANY—
ATLANTA, GA
Superintendent of Construction   Mar. 1987–Jan. 1991

NAS CONSTRUCTION COMPANY—ORLANDO, FL
Owner operator   Mar. 1983–Mar. 1987

INTERNATIONAL HARVESTER COMPANY—
ORLANDO, FL
Quality Control Inspector   1982–1983

EDUCATION

Florida State University—Tallahassee, FL
> Bachelor of Science—1981 Biology major; Chemistry minor

Dade County Vo-Tech
> Building Trades—1975–1976

SEMINARS

Denis Waitley 1999

Brian Tracy
> "Psychology of Success" July 1997

Media Images
> Jan. 1989–Mar. 1996

Kenneth Blanchard
> "The One Minute Manager" 1993

Adventure Works
> "The 48 Hour Adventure" 1992

REFERENCES

Available upon request

This writer has technical construction skills and is building directly on past experience.

Bob Francis   *Résumé of Qualifications*
367 Old Hickory Blvd.
White House, Tennessee 37189 (615) 931-4507

SKILLS
SUMMARY   More than 24 years experience in construction, including management/super-
                 vision, estimating, and purchasing. Working knowledge of drafting, carpentry,
                 and welding, with excellent troubleshooting and problem-solving skills.

PROFESSIONAL
EXPERIENCE   **FOREMOST CONSTRUCTION** Nashville, TN
                 July 1998–Present
                 Licensed Contractor #00036484

                 HARDAWAY CONSTRUCTION Nashville, TN
                 April 1995–July 1998
                 Journeyman Carpenter

                 MILLWORKS INTERNATIONAL Nashville, TN
                 Feb. 1991–April 1995
                 Manager: Estimating, Purchasing,
                 Designing Cabinetry, Supervising
                 cabinet makers.

                 FLOUR DANIEL SERVICES CORP. Greenville, SC
                 March 1990–May 1991
                 Journeyman Carpenter: Read blueprints,
                 shot elevations, operated manlifts,
                 and supervised concrete pouring.

                 FRANCIS CABINETS Joelton, TN
                 Feb. 1984–March 1990
                 Owner/Operator: Responsibilities
                 included all sales, estimates,
                 drafting, purchasing, and collecting.

                 HAURY & SMITH
                 CONSTRUCTION COMPANY Nashville, TN
                 Jan. 1983–Feb. 1984
                 Trim Carpenter

EDUCATION   **TENNESSEE STATE UNIVERSITY** 1991–1994
                 NASHVILLE AREA VOCATIONAL SCHOOL
                 (Welding—496 Hrs.) (Architectural
                 Draftsman Detailer—676 Hrs.)

REFERENCES   Available upon request

This writer is a sales professional, building from past employer experience.

WILLIAM W. BARNETTE JR.
110 St. Andrews Drive
Rome, GA 37064
(713) 646-3274

SKILLS SUMMARY

Solid experience in consultative outside-selling, promoting, and concept marketing. Competent in planning, organizing, and creating strategic plans with distributors. Committed to high work-ethics and attainment of sales goals. Proven skills in territory management and the ability to increase sales. Comfortable negotiating agreements with win/win outcomes.

PROFESSIONAL EXPERIENCE

1985–Present   **COOPER INDUSTRIES, INC. (CROUSE-HINDS ECM DIVISION)**
Sales Representative
Market-wide range of specialty products to Industrials, OEMs, and electrical contractors. Responsibilities include establishing product specifications with design engineers while generating increased sales. Coordinate market planning, product training meetings, stock analysis, and new product introductions. Budget has expanded 250 percent over 4 years to $2.5 million while budget goals have been achieved each year. Increased current territory sales by 25 percent. Promoted to Senior Sales in 1987.

1984–1985   **GENERAL ELECTRIC COMPANY**
Customer Service Representative
Coordinated inside sales responsibilities to OEM accounts representing 3 million in sales in 1984. Provided technical assistance, negotiated pricing, generated technical quotations in addition to scheduling sales orders.

1983–1984   **CHAMPION INTERNATIONAL, INC.**
Sales Service Representative
Sold forest products for Fortune 500 company through selected building materials distributors. Inside sales responsibilities included inventory control of satellite distribution center and purchase of selected products.

1981–1982   **B-LINE SYSTEMS, INC.**
Outside Sales
Promoted to outside sales after 8 months in territory of North and South Carolina. Sold through electrical distributors. Responsible for product specifications at major industrial accounts and engineering firms.

EDUCATION   B.S.—Georgia Institute of Technology, 1981
Major: Industrial Management

REFERENCES Excellent references available upon request

This gentleman had been out of the workforce for 3 years with a triple organ transplant. We drew from competencies of work experience prior to that time, but were able to cover the gaps and move on.

James Bronson
3856 Confederation Rd.
Nashville, Tennessee 37229
(615) 896-3464

SKILLS SUMMARY

Solid engineering experience in machining and fabricating manufacturing environments. Strong interpersonal skills and ability to interact positively with all levels of management. Proven skills in technical design and systems, balanced with people-management ability. Committed to high work-ethics and to attainment of management goals and objectives.

RELEVANT SKILLS AND EXPERIENCE

MANAGEMENT

Capable of building strong teams for maximum use of people resources. Skilled at negotiating and resolving employee needs. Able to select, manage, and motivate people for efficient production. Served as liaison between engineering and manufacturing. Responsible for quality and schedule performance. Competent in assessing risk factors.

PROJECT COORDINATION

Implemented and installed CAD/CAM/CIM system. Responsible for government regulations and DOD testing requirements. Quite familiar with quality issues and requirements, including MIL-STD 9858, Ford's Q-101, and GM's Targets For Excellence. Oversaw purchasing, JIT, Kanban logic, statistical process control, time measurement, and inventory control. Proficient at job costing, quoting, and processing.

ENGINEERING

Designed flow of work for innovative engine design (Ford's MOD-3 Modular Engine). Facilitated machining changes and personally suggested improvements. Strong background in automotive engineering. Experienced with conventional machining, automatic screw machines, cold-forming, stamping, stretch-forming, CNC mills, and turning centers. Supervised and programmed CNC machined products relating to the fluid motion and fluid power industry, including hose fittings, connectors, and fasteners for the military, automotive, and OEM manufacturers.

PROFESSIONAL HISTORY

BLAIRS, INC. Nashville, TN 1997–Present

PARKER HANNIFIN CORPORATION Cleveland, OH
1990–1997

AVCO/TEXTRON AEROSTRUCTURES Nashville, TN
1987–1990

BETTY MACHINE CO. Nashville, TN 1985–1987

EDUCATION

B.S. Manufacturing Engineering Technology, MTSU, May 1995

A.S. Mechanical Engineering, July 1987

A.A. Industrial Engineering, March 1987

(Currently completing M.S. in Industrial Studies)

REFERENCES Available upon request

Note specifics in work history. The more specific you can be, the fewer the competitors, and the more likely you are to raise your salary range. You will also separate yourself from recent graduates, but also from those with perhaps more degrees and credentials.

Dorothy Newsom, P.E.
126 Riverwood Drive, Pittsburg, PA 24356
412-790-3487

PROFILE

Engineering/Project Management

Skills encompass engineering management, team leadership, and field project management. Background in industrial, commercial, petrochemical, and residential projects with involvement from concept development and initial client presentations through design/build to acceptance and preparation of proposed drawings. Extensive experience working with consultants (architectural, environmental, legal, governmental).

EXPERIENCE

SMITH AND WATSON, INC. Pittsburgh, PA   1996–Present

Principal Engineer

Selected Projects:

Field Engineer at Tooele, Utah, U.S. Army munitions storage plant. Resolved conflicts with design drawings and coordinated final design requirements. Provided detail for 100+ specially designed embedded wall plates that facilitated easy placement of concrete and expedited project.

Conducted inspections for ERMST (Earthquake Recovery Management Support Team) following the Northridge earthquake. Wrote reports for county, authorizing residential buildings to receive funds for reconstruction.

Conducted structural analysis using 3-D computer model for ARCO GHX-1 and GHX-2 steel-frame structures.

FLOUR-DANIEL/TRS, Philadelphia, PA   1988–1996

Civil/Structural Engineer

Managed FAA Golden Gate Airway Sector refurbishment project. Analyzed refurbishment needs for coming year and created and implemented site-specific solutions. Monitored annual budget of $9 million. Acted as liaison between field offices, site supervisors, and governmental agencies. Prepared budgets and cost estimates for projects and oversaw new construction.

Designed pre-engineered metal buildings for public, private, and commercial use.

Developed construction details that allowed metal-roof framing to accommodate masonry and tilt-up panel walls, significantly expanding product market and increasing sales.

BROWN AND LINSEY, Hershey, PA   1985–1988

Project Engineer

Lead structural engineer for creation on concrete and steel structures for refinery and chemical plants. Oversaw 4 engineers in pipe-support group. Constructed 3-D computer models to analyze various structures. Designed plant facilities and modification of existing facilities.

EDUCATION

UNIVERSITY OF TENNESSEE, Knoxville, TN
Bachelor of Science, Civil Engineering
CREDENTIALS
State of Pennsylvania Civil Engineer No. C03787345
State of Pennsylvania Structural Engineer No. S099743
AFFILIATIONS
Member, Structural Engineers Association of Pennsylvania
Pittsburgh Chamber of Commerce
Women in Business, National Association

REFERENCES
Available upon request

1615 North Chapel Road, Atlanta, GA (513) 748-9852
Deborah Turner

Marketing—Advertising—Communications

Professional Profile   Creative, self-motivated, professional with 13 years experience in marketing and business management. Skilled at communication and customer service. Adept problem-solver with proven ability to coordinate projects including graphic design and promotional components.

Summary

- Built advertising department for retail clothing store as company's first marketing director.
- Reorganized and centralized marketing functions of 10 regional banks following merger, increasing budget efficiencies by 28 percent.
- Oversaw development of corporate training videos.
- Secured statewide press coverage in *Atlanta Journal* for promotional rollout.
- Coordinated fundraising for Muscular Dystrophy annual walkathon, raising an 18-year high in funds and participation.
- Designed direct-mail campaign for successful state senator race.

Career Highlights

Advertising Coordinator   Samantha's Fashions Atlanta, GA
- Expanded territorial sales by 400 percent.
- Received company's highest sales award four years in a row.

Marketing Director   Regions Bank, Inc.   Atlanta, GA
- Coordinated merger marketing and public relations campaign
- Controlled $2 million advertising budget.
- Developed Excellence in Sales training course.

Muscular Dystrophy Association South Ridge, GA
- Directed fund-raising and promotional awareness, including all media.

Education and Training

- B.A., Business Administration and Marketing
University of Georgia
- Graduated summa cum laude.

References   Available upon request

HELEN DRISCOLL

Mt. Washington, New Jersey 09675 Phone: (512) 291-1404 Email: info@comcast.net

CAREER FOCUS:
ANALYST / PROGRAMMER

Team-oriented, quality-focused IT professional with experience as a software engineer and programmer analyst for new systems and system enhancements in diverse industries.
Expertise includes:

Systems Analysis   Coding   Program Specifications   Data Mapping Requirements   Online and Batch Programs   SPUFIs   Test Scripts   Testing Support

PROFESSIONAL EXPERIENCE

PARSONS COMPUTER PROFESSIONALS, INC.—Cranford, New Jersey   September 2001 to January 2003

STAFF CONSULTANT

Programming consultant working at client site (Vanguard Group) for this global IT outsourcing/contracting firm. Served on eight-person, cross-functional project teams performing program development, enhancements, and testing for several of Vanguard's financial services information systems. Developed program specifications, test scripts, SPUFIs, DB2 batch programs and data mapping requirements. Utilized DB2, COBOL2, CICS, MVS JCL, VSAM (legacy system), Microfocus Mainframe Express, Endeavor and other technologies.

Project Highlights
- Delivered outstanding results under strict deadlines in ever-changing environments. Maintained excellent track record of client satisfaction and on-time assignment completion.
- Managed code editing and process corrections and developed transaction engine for large enhancement (Vanguard Brokerage Option Phase 2), a product which allows Vanguard clients independently to transfer investments between portfolios when changing employers. Took responsibility for an additional project section that was in jeopardy, successfully completed assignments on time and restored relations with client's DBA staff.
- Wrote programs and code for tables for system that would make a number of client's smaller systems obsolete.

ALUNION FINANCIAL—Worcester, Massachusetts   1996 to 2001

SOFTWARE ENGINEER

Software engineer performing maintenance and developing ad hoc programs and enhancements on the Vantage Annuity System for this financial services company. Served as primary point of contact for IT staff and brokers in the field for a large system with hundreds of subprograms. Held full responsibility for disaster recovery testing. Gained knowledge of writing DB2 SPUFIs and writing in different languages.

• Independently developed online and batch process for creating TSA (Tax Shelter Annuities) definitions and letters, requiring changes to, or writing of, 15 programs.

• Created batch process for data extract for Electronic Data Interface (EDI) feed from Annuities system to DSTFanmail and NSCC. Analyzed and reorganized nightly job schedule to include several parallel jobs running simultaneously and supervised third-shift computer operators to ensure successful project completion.

• Ensured Y2K readiness for the Repetitive Payment System. Performed system analysis, developed test plan, prepared program modification specifications, and supervised contractors to complete project on time.

• Selected to chair department's Employee of the Month committee.

NEW ENGLAND POWER SERVICE COMPANY—Westboro, Massachusetts 1991 to 1996

ASSOCIATE INFORMATION ANALYST
Developed programs and enhancements for numerous IT systems, including timekeeping, payroll, accounting, and fleet management for this large utility company. Utilized numerous technologies including EasyTrieve Plus, COBOL2, and DB2.

• Successfully completed challenging project for time entry system using IEF language despite no prior experience with the language. Met severe time constraints and worked in adverse conditions in a mobile office. Survived four different project leaders within eight months to become SME on the system.

EDUCATION

BOSTON UNIVERSITY—Boston, Massachusetts
Bachelor of Science, Business Administration
Concentration: Management Information Systems

TECHNICAL SKILLS

COBOL2
COBOL
DB2
EasyTrieve Plus
QMF
SQL
EDI Entry
EDI Developer
CICS
MVS JCL
VSAM
TSO/ISPF
Microfocus Mainframe Express
Endeavor
File Aid
MS Office

James C. Tanner

512.291.1404 • info@bellsouth.net *New Rochelle, New Jersey 09678*

Target • Career-focused Information Systems generalist seeking entry-level Visual Basic programming opportunity.

Strengths • Microsoft Certified Professional credential—Designing and implementing desktop applications with MS Visual Basic 6.0

• OS Expertise: Windows 9x/2000/XP . . . AS400

• Logic & Flowcharting . . . RDBMS . . . C / C++ . . . Java . . . Activate X Controls

• SQL . . . VBA . . . HTML . . . RPG/400 . . . COBOL II . . . FORTRAN

• Program design and development integrating Visual Basic with MS Access, using the database in the interface, and retrieving data using SQL statements

Value-added

Attributes

• Mature, energetic, and highly professional. Flexible and adaptable—willing to work overtime, odd shifts, or on an on-call basis to deliver superior, clean and readable code under tight deadlines.

• Logical thinking, detail-oriented perfectionist—highly suited to performing exacting analytical work under intensive time pressures.

• Outstanding communication, information gathering and focused listening skills—competent in asking appropriate questions to effectively and completely understand assignment or critical need and deliver expected results.

• Willing to exercise initiative, take on increased responsibilities, learn new skills independently, and maintain good working relationships by demonstrating a sense of humor and interpersonal respect for coworkers.

Programming

Experience

  Programming Intern • November 1999 to March 2000

THE JOHNSON CORPORATION, Three Rivers, Michigan

• Worked directly with VP of Research & Development (R&D) and in close collaboration with internal R&D professionals to design critical interface allowing end users (sales personnel) to input up to five data sets and accurately and rapidly process vast amounts of complex scientific data on site for customers in the paper manufacturing industry.

• Sole applications programmer on project. Developed stand-alone, Visual Basic 5.0 application featuring nested-if statement validity checking for ten different pressure, temperature, and flow conditions; a series of Error Message displays; ten types of pressure, temperature, and flow labels; and a comprehensive report generation and printing function.

• Net results: Program reduced time required to calculate raw data and streamlined storage of technical data.

Advanced Technical
Training
Programming Degree Track • October 2002 (4.00 GPA)
BRICK COMPUTER SCIENCE INSTITUTE, Brick, New Jersey
• Mastered techniques required to design, write, implement, debug, enhance, and maintain business software applications on PC platforms through extensive classroom-based instruction and applied-learning opportunities involving real-world programming methodologies. Featured projects include: Database Management: Programmed two-version releases of a Visual Basic frontend / MS Access back end application. Executed all critical aspects of validity checking, screen design, work flow-charting/planning, etc.
Game development: Incorporated several different games into one user authenticated, password-protected application. Executed story planning, developed menu systems, and designed task bars, programming entire package (2 games and 1 splash/intro game) in Visual Basic 6.0.

Education
KALAMAZOO VALLEY COMMUNITY COLLEGE, Kalamazoo, Michigan
Computer Information Systems • 2001 (with Honors; GPA: 3.80)
Mathematics • 1993 (with Honors; GPA: 3.86)
MONMOUTH UNIVERSITY, West Long Branch, New Jersey
Bachelor of Science—Elementary Education

Interim
Employment
Team Captain • July 2001 to Present
MERRY MAIDS, INC., Rochelle Park, New Jersey
•Lead multiperson teams in performing at or above franchise standards.
Bakery Clerk • November 1999 to March 2000
MORRISONS, INC., Princeton, Michigan
•Worked part-time for this supermarket chain while attending college.

Teaching
Career
Elementary Instructor • 1990 to 1997
THE MONTESSORI SCHOOL, Kansas City, Missouri
Elementary Instructor • 1988 to 1990
NEW HORIZONS MONTESSORI SCHOOL, Philadelphia, Pennsylvania
Summary
•Deliberate career changer unafraid of taking risks to learn new skills and enhance career prospects. Willing to absorb relocation expenses.

Now, you are ready to construct or revise your own résumé. Don't make this process more complex than it needs to be. Spend 1 to 2 hours and complete it. Yes, it needs to be great, but it's still only maybe 15 percent of the process. Your creative job search, introduction letters, cover letters, phone follow-up, and interviewing skills are equally important components. Create your own look or choose one of the résumé templates found on any word processing system.

Then you are ready to move on.

Chapter Eight

Creative Job Search Strategy

The most effective job-hunting method is this: know your skills, research the potential companies that use those skills, arrange to see the person who has the power to hire you, and request the interview. This method, faithfully followed, leads to a job for 86 out of every 100 job hunters who use it.

Compare this to:

1. Answering local newspaper ads leads to jobs for about 8 out of 100. (The higher the level the job you seek, the less effective this method is.)

2. Private employment agencies and headhunter pursuits lead to jobs for 4 to 22 out of 100. (Again, depending on the level sought.) No one can present you as well as you can or cares about your situation as much as you do.

3. Answering ads in trade journals leads to jobs for 7 out of 100. (Too much time delay, etc.)

4. Mass response to Internet ads. The ads at Monster.com or HotJobs.com look so perfect to you. Just keep in mind that whatever you see, thousands of other great candidates see as well. While there are exceptions to everything, the results here are pretty dismal. Fewer than 1 percent of job seekers actually get a position from responding to an Internet ad. (Most people using the Internet as their primary job search tool are simply hiding out, avoiding real contact, and wasting time.)

Other methods that are even better than those common ones:

5. Applying directly to an employer without doing any homework leads to a job for 47 out of 100. Just walking in the door, unannounced, works almost half the time. Notice, this is the second most effective method but works best for lower-level positions.

6. Asking friends for job leads gets a job for 34 out of 100 who try it. Don't be hesitant about letting others know what you are looking for.

7. Asking relatives for job leads gets a job for about 27 out of 100.

8. Using the placement office at the school or college you once attended leads to a job for 21 out of 100.

The major difference between successful and unsuccessful
job hunters is not skill, education, age, or ability but
the way they go about their job hunt.
(Perhaps the most important statement in this book!)

The old rule of thumb is that the job-hunt process takes 30 days for every $10,000 of compensation. Thus, a $60,000 position will take 6 months. This is a discouraging statistic. However, look at the figures that lead to such a generality. Most people in a job search are contacting 4 or 5 companies a month. At this rate of contact, yes, it may take 6 months. However, finding a position is a sales process and if you understand the numbers involved, you can dramatically increase your rate success.

If you are selling vacuum cleaners, you may know from the company history that 1 out of 23 contacts will lead to a sale. So then you can decide whether you will make those 23 contacts today or if you will make 1 contact each of the next 23 days. Your rate of making those contacts will determine the timing of your success. Keep in mind that your job search is much the same process. What I lay out here is a short 30-day burst of focused activity, leading to whatever level of compensation you desire in a much shorter period of time.

Two-thirds of all job hunters spend 5 hours or less on their job hunt each week, according to the US Census Bureau. If you are serious about seeking a new position, you cannot afford this rate of progress. My advice, based on seeing successful job hunters, is to spend 35 hours per week in the search. This will dramatically cut down the time in weeks and months to conduct a successful search.

THE JOB SEARCH PROCESS THAT WORKS!

This phase of the process is an intensive but short and focused process (if you are investing 35 hours per week.) And don't think you can't complete this process while you are working. You can. Most people in a job search today are currently employed. Everything but the interviews

 "LOW WAGES, LOW HOURS"

"Men wanted for hazardous journey. Low wages, long hours." This ad was placed in the early 1900s by the explorer Ernest Shackleton as he was looking for men to help him discover the South Pole. The ad drew more than 5,000 brave candidates.

Are you looking for a "safe" and "stable" position today? One that is secure, predictable and non-threatening? Maybe you're missing the best opportunities. I truly believe that if defeat or failure is not possible, then winning will not be sweet.

A missionary society wrote to David Livingston deep in the heart of Africa and asked: "Have you found a good road to where you are? If so, we want to know how to send other men to help you." Livingston wrote back: "If you have men who will come only if they know there is a good road, I don't want them. I want men who will come if there is no road at all."

themselves can be done without interfering with a normal work day. You simply need to see it as a short burst of intensive energy to lead you to the future you want.

THE FOUR CRITICAL STEPS OF THE JOB SEARCH

1. Identify thirty to forty target companies. Do you want a place with 20 to 85 employees? A profit or nonprofit organization? A manufacturing or service company? A new company or an old established one? Do you want to travel or be home every evening? An organization in health, retail, finances, entertaining, printing, etc. Use your city's business directory, the Chamber of Commerce directory, an industry guide (readily available at your local library for media, manufacturing, non-profits, etc.) to help you create this target list. (Most libraries will have both local and national search tools for selecting companies based on your search criteria.)

You are in the driver's seat to choose the companies you would like to work with. You don't have to wait until a company advertises a position or you hear someone say that a company is hiring. Those usual methods typically put you up against 70 to 80 people for almost any desirable position, whereas in this method you may have 2 to 3 competitors. You must recognize that when you see an ad for a particular position, you have already lost your best opportunity for that position. Also, this is the method for finding the 87 percent of the jobs that are never advertised. In a rapidly changing workplace, everyone is looking for good people. Be proactive in your search.

2. Send a letter of introduction to each company. (Send no more than 15 at a time so you can do the appropriate follow-up.) The letter of introduction is just to build name recognition. (See the sample introduction letter that follows this section.)

3. Send your cover letter and résumé 1 week after your introduction letter. Address the cover letter to a specific person. You can get this name from the Business Directory or by calling the company. Receptionists are wonderful about giving useful information if you ask nicely. Don't bother sending the letter to the "Personnel Department," "Human Resources," or "To Whom It May Concern." Target a person who can make a hiring decision. That's normally going to be the sales manager, the vice president of operations, the president, the office manager, etc.

4. Follow up with a phone call. This step is very important. My experience is that only about 1 to 2 percent of job hunters do this. It is easy to bring your name to the top of the list if you just make a follow-up call. Don't be afraid of being persistent! Call 4 to 5 days after sending résumé. In the phone call say, "This is Bill Smith. I'm following up on a recent letter and résumé. I know what your company does and really think I could add to your success. When can we get together and talk?" You'll be surprised how frequently people will say, "Why don't you come by tomorrow at 2:00?"

Keep in mind that if you just send cover letters and résumés, you need to send out 254 to have a statistical chance of getting a job offer. If you combine that with a phone call, the number drops to 1 out of 15—a dramatic difference. Add to that an introduction letter and the results will amaze you. This is a selling process. We use a 3-time repetitive process because of understanding marketing principles. If you are selling recliners, having someone see or hear about them three times will increase their response. In this process you are selling a product, and that product is you! Just commit to the process and a time line.

This process, if followed precisely, does get results. A gentleman who sent out more than 1,000 résumés over a 14-month period with no job offers was able to get 5 interviews with 3 offers in a 45-day period using this method. Another client who had gone 6 months with no interviews received 4 offers in 10 days with this system. A recent college graduate with no real work experience received 6 job offers in a 10-day period using this process. Remember, no one is going to come looking for you. You must do an active, aggressive search. It's not uncommon for competent professionals to resist the aggressive nature of an effective job search. They tend to assume that their credentials and great work history will speak for itself and that pushing for contacts and interviews is somehow less than professional. Unfortunately, we are in a marketing environment. No longer is it true that if you "build a better mousetrap, people will beat a path to your door." A clear plan of "selling" is required to find success in any arena. Finding a great job is no exception!

IMPORTANT NOTE: Again, don't think that I am ignoring the possibilities with the Internet. Yes, I know you can get the e-mails of 10,000 Human Resource directors and have your wonderful résumé in their mailbox this afternoon. However, I also know that 9,999 of them will resent your intrusion. And we know now that 75 percent of the companies that have hired from the Internet have had a bad experience. We are seeing a swing back to the traditional face-to-face process for effective hiring. A professional, printed copy of your résumé in a real envelope is still the most respected method of first contact.

An irony in low unemployment times is that you may tend to think that if a company advertises a position, you are probably the only person who responded, and they will call on Monday and ask you to start work on Tuesday. That is absolutely false. Even in low unemployment, they will receive

---

 ## DEALING WITH JOB SEARCH DISCOURAGEMENT

You wouldn't be human if you didn't feel discouragement while you are unemployed. We attach too much of our worth and self-esteem to our jobs, and, consequently, when we are "inbetween opportunities," it's natural to feel anxious at times. But you do have daily choices: you can convince yourself you are looking into an empty future, or you can believe that a better opportunity awaits you. I frequently tell clients that the distance between terror and exhilaration, between hope and hopelessness is often a fine line. Remember that frustration in or even losing a job may simply be God's prod to go on to a higher level of success. Here are 10 tips on how to cope after a job loss:

1. Find selective places to talk honestly about your feelings.
2. Increase your knowledge about the job-search process.
3. Define what you can and cannot control.
4. Live each day fully. Take a fresh look at the success you have in areas other than work.
5. Do something for someone else. Volunteer time to worthy causes or organizations.
6. Build your own support system. Ask for help. Don't hide out in the library all day and never let your neighbors know you are looking.
7. Do something creative. Joanne and I sometimes work on big jigsaw puzzles. You'll find energy for the search if you give yourself creative breaks.
8. Maintain exercise and good nutrition.
9. Maintain hope and optimism. Set achievable daily and weekly goals. Do physical projects where you can see the results immediately.
10. Look for the larger meaning in this transition process.

70 to 80 responses. That tells us that although most people are working, many of those people are in the job market. They know there are many new opportunities, so they are looking as well.

Everything prior to the interview is preliminary. No one will hire you from a résumé, nor do you want them to. Résumés and the active job search lead to interviews. Interviews get you the job.

Time spent on a good job search is time invested in your future. Don't view it casually. A week spent researching a couple of key companies so that you are more knowledgeable in the interview could mean a difference of thousands of dollars in your income in the next 2 to 3 years alone.

The average job in America now lasts 3.2 years. The average American worker will therefore have 14 to 16 different jobs in his/her working lifetime. Learn how to do this process well. You will have to do it again. Knowing this process will serve you well in the inevitable future changes. Recognize that you must take responsibility for the success of the process. No one can do it for you—not the government, the state, the church, or any agency. All of these are attempts to avoid your own responsibility. Be prepared to deal with rejection and then continue being persistent, confident that real success is just a few more contacts away!

For many of you, the job search strategy section will be the most important piece of information in this entire workbook. If you understand and follow this procedure, you can dramatically transform your results, bypassing other applicants with more degrees, credentials, and experience!

SAMPLE INTRODUCTION LETTER

The italicized headings below are not to be included on your letter but show you the issues to be addressed.

Mr. David C. Milton
BMI International, Inc.
7300 Franklin Road
Brentwood, TN 37027

Dear Mr. Milton:

Introduction: Current Situation/Goals: After more than 14 years as a sales professional in the medical field, I am exploring new opportunities where my sales abilities may continue to be used. Positions commensurate with my past experience and career goals would be:

> Manager of Training and Staff Development
> Manager of Human Resource Development
> Director of Sales and Marketing

What's Special about Me: My record is one of solid accomplishments and increasing levels of responsibility. The training programs I have developed have been adopted as a model for our company's 23 nationwide locations. My sales goals have been exceeded by an average of 34 percent in the last 5 years.

Next Step: I will forward my résumé to you in the next few days to allow you to explore how my qualifications may match growth opportunities in your company.

Sincerely,

Jason L. Smith

Notice this requires nothing of the recipient. It simply tells him/her what is going to happen next. And it plants the seed so your name begins to become familiar. We are in a culture where repetition sells, and in this process you want at least 3 exposures to create "top of mind" positioning.

SAMPLE COVER LETTER

Kevin A. Smith
3736 Mitchell Drive
Ft. Collins, Colorado 76809

November 30, 2002

Mr. William Fowler
Vice President of Sales
The Dixon Company
199 Commerce Way
Boulder, Colorado 76821

Dear Mr. Fowler:

With this letter, I wish to express my strong interest in working with the Dixon Company as a regional sales manager. After 7 years in sales management and customer service, I believe I would bring several areas of competence to the Dixon Company. Accordingly, a complete résumé detailing my professional background is enclosed for your review and consideration.

In my current position, it is my responsibility to recruit, motivate, and train my staff to ensure that high quality and desired goals are obtained. In addition, I oversee the business development of all new products with bottom-line accountability for established profit goals. It is also my responsibility to maintain the integrity of the account base through sound credit decisions.

In this assignment, I opened a branch in a new market and doubled the account base in 6 months, reaching 150 percent of the expected growth and 200 percent of the profit goal. I accomplished this by leading the staff in effectively cross-selling our product line and providing exceptional customer service. This is just one example of how the Dixon Company may benefit by our mutual alliance.

I would very much like to speak with you about the sales management opportunities and ways that you can use my expertise. Please expect my call on Wednesday, December 7, to arrange a convenient time to discuss that and more. I look forward to speaking with you then about opportunities in the Southwestern or Midwestern U.S.

Sincerely,

Kevin A. Smith
kas
Enclosure
You'll notice it does not say, "I look forward to hearing from you" or "Please call me at your earliest convenience." You must stay in the driver's seat.

SAMPLE FOLLOW-UP LETTER

Charles S. Miller
2503 Concord Lane
Lakeland, Florida 27064
(863) 453-7786

James R. Johnson
Executive Director, YMCA
Orlando, Florida 26459

Dear Mr. Johnson:

Thank you for the opportunity to interview for the Youth Development Coordinator position. I appreciate your consideration and interest in me.

As we discussed this afternoon, my experience and educational experience have prepared me well for this position. I have enjoyed the similar work I have been privileged to do both in my current position and through my church involvement.

I want to reiterate my strong interest in working with you and the Orlando YMCA. Please keep in mind my personal attraction to this work that goes beyond just my academic credentials. I trust this gives me an added component as an appropriate candidate.

Again, thank you for considering me for this opportunity to build positive characteristics in the lives of young people and the chance to serve our community. As we discussed, I will call you Thursday morning to check the status of your decision.

Sincerely,

Charles S. Miller

Notice the strong "selling" language still being presented. Don't be afraid to tell them you want the position and that you think you are the best candidate. If you aren't convinced of that, it will be difficult for the interviewer to believe it.

48 DAYS
Hall of Fame

Fourteen months ago Tony was a high level property manager with a well-established company. Then the company was acquired by a larger national organization. They eliminated all local people in the existing company. Tony had not been too concerned. After all, he was well respected and had many friends in the industry. For the first 60 days he simply waited for those phone calls he knew would come from his many contacts asking him to join their organizations. Seeing that time period pass rather quickly, Tony thought maybe he ought to send out a few resumes. Fourteen months flew by. Tony had now sent out more than a thousand resumes, responding to local and national newspaper ads, yet without a single interview. Panic set in. While previously used to a $70,000 salary, he was now willing to move anywhere and take a $20,000 position.

Tony was told we would not assist him in finding a $20,000 job, as that would be a temporary band-aid, sure to lead to frustration six months later. We would, however, help him correct his job search process to find the ideal position. Tony, while reluctant and impatient, agreed to begin a proper job search. In 45 days, after 14 months with no interviews, Tony had been interviewed 5 times and had been offered 3 positions, all at higher incomes than his previous high of $70,000.

The difference between successful and nonsuccessful job hunters is not skill, ability, education, age or experience as much as it is how they go about the job search process.

(See www.48Days.com.)

Chapter Nine

Preparing for the Interview

As we have already stated, the average job in America is now 3.2 years. The average American worker will thus have fourteen to sixteen different jobs in his/her working lifetime. Those positions are attained through the process of an interview, yet many job seekers fail to develop good interviewing skills. Interviews are commonly viewed as a necessary evil and are approached with a great deal of anxiety and apprehension.

Recognizing that change is inevitable and that "security" in the workplace no longer exists, it seems advisable to focus on developing interviewing skills so that these changes can be dealt with as smoothly as possible. Interviewing is a fine art and should be studied, prepared for, and practiced. One's ability to interview well will translate into job satisfaction and higher income.

Simply stated, a person who does not interview well will not receive a job offer. You may have an exceptional résumé and exceptional credentials and qualifications, but if you do not present well in the interview, you will not receive job offers. If you cannot present yourself with confidence and project a professional image in the interview, all your preparation will have been in vain. *You must develop and practice your interviewing skills.*

Remember that in the process of a job search, you are marketing yourself. If you are uncomfortable with selling, you must prepare yourself for this process. You must present yourself with knowledge about, belief in, and enthusiasm for the product.

Contrary to popular belief, the interview is not designed to be an inquisition or interrogation. The word *interview* is derived from a Latin word that means "to see about each other." It is important to keep this definition in mind when interviewing. "To see about each other" implies that an interview is a mutual exchange of information. This exchange process not only provides the employer with the opportunity to assess your skills and qualifications, but it also provides you with the opportunity to evaluate the company/organization and proposed position to determine if it matches your qualifications and needs.

Do not view the interview as a one-sided process. If you are completing a well-planned job search strategy, you will have several interviews leading to 2 to 3 job offers. The interview should be an information-gathering process for you as well as the interviewer. The keys to successful interviewing are preparation, knowing what to expect, and practice. Yes, practice is a reasonable ingredient. Most of us do not interview often enough to become proficient at it. Recognizing that interviewing skills translate into satisfaction and income, you would be well advised to practice as you would at improving your golf or tennis game.

PREPARATION, PREPARATION, PREPARATION

Preparation is the single most important factor in successful interviews. Your preparation should involve 2 primary components: *knowing yourself and knowing the company.*

KNOWING YOURSELF

Critical to presenting yourself well and securing a position that will be meaningful and fulfilling is the process of self-assessment. You should be intimately familiar with your skills and abilities, your personality tendencies, and your values, dreams, and passions. Only by having a clear understanding of these areas will you be prepared to search in a targeted, focused direction. Obtaining a job is your goal; however, be sure that what is required in the position—and the environment connected with it—are a good fit for you, your abilities, and your interests.

Be prepared in this regard to answer the following questions in the interview: (more questions will be presented later, but these few are critical in thoroughly knowing yourself)

1. "Tell me a little about yourself."

This is a standard question in nearly every interview. In some ways, it is probably the most important question in your interview, and you *must* prepare your answer well in advance. The interviewer will expect you to have developed an answer for this question, and if you have not, you will appear ill-prepared, and the interview will be off to a poor start.

This is your opportunity to sell yourself. Tell the interviewer what you want him to remember about you. You can refer to information you may want to bring up later in the interview.

An interviewer can quickly determine if you are knowledgeable and prepared or just another *wandering generality* hoping to land any job.

Your answer to any question should be no more than 2 minutes in length. On this particular one, you might spend 15 seconds on your personal background, 1 minute on your career highlights, a few seconds on your strongest professional achievement, and then conclude by explaining why you are looking for a new opportunity.

Ask yourself, "What can I contribute to this company?" and let that guide your response. Regardless of the content of your answer, you should outline the answer to this question on paper then practice it many times until you can repeat it concisely. Ask a friend or spouse to listen and critique it for you.

2. What are 3 of your strengths?

If you cannot clearly identify and describe your strengths, how do you expect an interviewer to pull them out in the brief encounter of an interview?

3. Tell me about a weakness and what you have done to work on it.

Don't play ignorant or modestly claim perfection. Be prepared to talk about something you struggle with. At the same time, stay positive in regard to what you have done to improve.

4. What skills do you possess that have prepared you for this job?

Obviously, you need to have researched the company and the job, or you will be unprepared for this question. Again, self-assessment should have made clear identification of your skill areas and competencies.

5. What are your short- and long-range goals?

Talk about personal goals as well as business goals. Companies today are looking for balanced individuals who are interested in things other than work. Feel free to share these goals. Talk about opportunity to move up in the company if that is your true desire, but don't say you want to be president.

More questions will be presented in a later section. These are shown here to help you look at knowing yourself.

KNOWING THE COMPANY

Knowledge of the company or organization, its products and services, its standing in the community, and the key individuals involved is essential. In addition, you should obtain information about the company's annual growth rate, annual sales, number of employees, location of the company headquarters, its major changes such as buyouts or mergers, and industry trends. The information you have, which will lead to questions you can ask, can easily tip the scales in your favor during the interview.

The following sources will help you in locating company information:

- Annual reports—available for the asking from any major company
- Business periodicals (*Wall Street Journal, Forbes, Fortune*, etc.)
- Industry magazines
- *Dun's Regional Business Directory*
- City business directory (available in any major city, it lists size, year started, number of employees, and contact principals)
- *Hoovers Business Directory* (get all the business directory information and more; latest stock quotes, quarterly earnings, SEC filings, compensation figures, etc.) at www.hoovers.com
- Moody's Manuals
- Standard & Poor's Publications
- *Standard & Poor's Register of Directors & Executives*
- *Thomas Register of American Manufacturer's Annual Reports*
- Better Business Bureau reports
- Chamber of Commerce publications
- Current employees (a valuable source for obtaining information)
- Bank of America Small *Business Resource Centers* (a wonderful resource for in-depth information about any company or organization in the United States)

Most of these reference materials can be found in any major library. Many also can be accessed on the Internet. Find the business section in a library and then ask for assistance. Librarians are normally eager to help and will make the use of your time more efficient.

OTHER COMPONENTS OF THE INTERVIEW PROCESS

THE DAY OF THE INTERVIEW

Ten seconds after you've walked into the room, before you even get a chance to sit down, you may have won or lost the job. While you may courteously be given an hour to answer questions and describe your accomplishments, studies indicate the interviewer forms a strong positive or negative impression of you within seconds of greeting you. One university study had job interviewers indicate when they had made a decision by pushing a button on a timer. *Every interviewer pushed the timer within 10 seconds.* This lets us know it's not the fine print on the fourth page of your résumé but other factors that take precedence in making the hiring decision.

After that first decision, interviewers tend to gather information to support the decision they have already made. A recent article in the *Nashville Business Journal* was titled "Making First Impressions Last." This article clarified that the purpose of a résumé is to obtain an interview, but no one hires from a résumé. The interview is where the rubber meets the road. In these first few minutes of an interview, the employer is asking, "Do I like this person? Do I trust this person? Is this person fun to be around?" Although it may be camouflaged, this is where the focus lies more than "Does this person have an MBA in marketing?"

With this in mind, here are some suggestions to help you create a positive impression.

TIME AND PLACE

1. The interviewer will schedule the time for the interview and the place where it will be conducted. If you are allowed to choose the time, avoid Monday mornings and Friday afternoons. Choose morning appointments. Executives found that 83 percent are more likely to hire job seekers in the morning. Appointments should be scheduled before 11:00 a.m. Afternoon appointments should be set no later than 1 hour prior to the close of the normal business day.

2. Know the exact time and location of the interview.

3. Be punctual; arrive 5 to 15 minutes early. Don't go in too early, but arrive early enough so you have the opportunity to observe the environment and determine if you would enjoy working there. (Interviewers will be annoyed as much by your arriving very early as by arriving late. Do neither.) To arrive too early indicates overanxiousness; to arrive late is inconsiderate. The only sensible solution is to arrive at the interview on time but at the location early. That allows you time to visit the restroom and make any necessary adjustments to your comfort and appearance. Take a couple of minutes to relax and prepare mentally.

4. Know the name and title of the interviewer. Do not use first names unless asked.

DRESS, APPEARANCE, AND ETIQUETTE

We have already established that an interviewer decides within the first few minutes whether he or she likes you. While some of the reasons may be subtle and intangible, we can control some of the more obvious ones to our advantage. The impression you want to create for the interviewer is directly reflected in the way you dress and in the way you handle yourself. Therefore, appropriate dress, mannerisms, and behavior are important variables.

1. Appropriate dress for the interview. There is only one way to dress for the first meeting: clean cut and conservative. You may not see yourself that way, and you know your right to look otherwise, but this is not the time to make a statement about your rights. *Your task is to understand how others see you.*

- Hair should be trimmed neatly.
- Shower or bathe as close to the interview time as possible. Use deodorant but not aftershave or perfume. You are trying to get hired, not courted.
- Be conservative on jewelry. Do not appear ostentatious or flamboyant.

- Make sure your shoes are neat and shined. Avoid worn belts, frayed collars, and ragged pockets.
- Use a small breath mint if you have a bad taste in your mouth. If you smoke, by all means, use a mint. Be aware that cigarette smoke permeates your clothing and hair. A strong odor may be offensive to a prospective employer.

Women

Professional, tailored clothes are best. This is not the time to make a fashion statement; just be professional. Do not carry both a notebook and a purse. For questions and note taking, carry a notebook small enough to fit easily into your handbag.

Men

Wear a well-pressed, conservative suit. Now certainly, if you were interviewing for a lawn maintenance position, this would not be necessary. However, always err on the side of overdressing, if you are unsure.

2. Warm-up or rapport building. The interviewer may initiate some small talk about noncontroversial matters. Many times the interviewer will find something on your résumé to talk about. Warm-up topics may include weather, sports, or one of your hobbies. The purpose of this warm-up is to help you feel relaxed and to develop a comfortable atmosphere so you will be able to speak freely and spontaneously about yourself. Remember, however, that from the first instant, you are being evaluated, even if you are not covering issues pertinent to the position.

3. Etiquette. Try to make the interview as comfortable as possible. Sit straight in the chair, be relaxed, and do not fidget. Use a firm, moderate tone when speaking. Make direct eye contact with the interviewer. Few things will sabotage your efforts quicker than poor eye contact. This is always perceived as shifty and dishonest. Watch your language. Obviously, avoid profanity or off-color comments. Avoid slang or cultural colloquialisms ("fixin', I done this, ain't nobody"). These may appear cute on television but are seen as unprofessional in the real world.

4. Body language. Think "up." Prior to the interview, focus on being "up" and on having your body language reflect being up. Keep your head up, your shoulders up, and your body straight. This posture sends a positive message, conveying energy and enthusiasm. Match your energy with that of the person interviewing you. It's OK to be confident and to speak up. You can have energetic body language. Don't come across as condescending or intimidating, but do be confident.

According to research, body language is 55 percent of the communication process. Communication can be enhanced or hindered by standing too close or too far away or being too animated or frigid.

Tone of voice is 38 percent of the communication process. Excessive tone ranges, loudness, or softness can open or close the doorway of communication.

Words make up only 7 percent of the communication process. The proper words can effectively communicate your message but only with proper body language and tone of voice.

- Practice your handshake. A weak handshake indicates a weak personality. Reach for full palm-to-palm contact. Don't offer just fingers.
- Make good eye contact immediately when you meet and when you shake hands. Weak or shifting eye contact is a sure sign of weakness, insecurity, or lack of confidence.

- Sit comfortably in the chair. Don't get too relaxed and slouch down. Sit straight and lean forward slightly. This shows interest and energy. When you are excited about something you are relating and you want to show you are "charged," lean forward in your chair. When you want to show that you are knowledgeable and confident, then you should lean back, and that will indicate your expertise. Sit with your arms comfortably in your lap or on the chair arms. Do not cross your arms; this is universally seen as closing off or holding back.
- Do not put your hands to your mouth. This is perceived as deceptive or trying to hide the truth. Avoid repetitive gestures. Avoid pointing or any excessive movements.
- Be aware of unique personal habits. (I recently interviewed a client with an annoying, sucking-sound laugh, which she offered approximately every 30 seconds. She was totally taken aback when I mentioned it and was genuinely unaware of its effect.)
- Do not be uncomfortable with silence. Experienced interviewers may purposely allow silence to see how you respond. Use the silence to rehearse what you may want to offer or what you may want to ask.

QUESTION AND ANSWER SECTION

The question-and-answer section usually takes up approximately 75 percent of the interview process. The candidate is asked to review his or her qualifications as presented on the résumé. (Remember that anything presented on the résumé is fair game, so be ready to discuss it. Thus, it's important to have on your résumé *only* items that act as sales tools for where you want to go.) After questions about your qualifications and skills, the interviewer will provide you with information about the company. Ideally, you then will be given an opportunity to ask questions. By all means, have 4 or 5 questions ready to ask. The questions you ask may create more of an impression than how you answered the previous ones. (Sample questions to ask will be given later in this workbook.)

EXITING THE INTERVIEW

As you prepare to leave, stand up straight and tall, shake hands, and then pick up your notebook. Make sure the exiting handshake is strong. Practice what you are going to say. Don't be afraid to ask what the next step will be. Have a closing well rehearsed. Ask, "What will be the next step? When can I expect a decision to be made? May I call you on Thursday?" Keep your body oriented toward the interviewer even as you are leaving. Continue to make eye contact until you turn to exit. Do not ask about salary and benefits at this time. Summarize your qualifications. Also, state whether you do or do not still want the job. Use this wrap-up as a time to show the interviewer that you have listened and heard what has been said about the company and the position. Make a closing statement that ties in all the information you have obtained from the interview.

GENERAL RULES TO REMEMBER!

1. Smile! Few things convey pleasantness, enthusiasm, and comfort like a smile. Successful people smile a lot. People who frown are not perceived as happy, productive professionals.

2. Be pleasant and outgoing. Do not attempt to take over the interview but respond easily and spontaneously to questions and the interview process.

3. Show self-confidence. Fidgeting, nervousness, glancing down, not accepting compliments, and self-deprecating statements convey poor self-confidence.

LOUDER THAN WORDS

We are seeing increasing creativity in interviewing today—on both sides. Many interviewers have a favorite question: "Why are manhole covers round? How many barbers are there in Chicago? If you could be an animal, what would it be?" Some interviewers are big on nonverbal clues as we are told that 55 percent of communication is nonverbal.

J. C. Penney was famous for taking potential hires out to breakfast. If that person put salt and pepper on his food before tasting it, the interview was over. Mr. Penney believed that such actions revealed a person who made decisions before he had all the evidence.

Jeff O'Dell of August Technology often asks candidates out to lunch and suggests that they drive. "How organized someone's car is an amazing indicator of how organized the rest of his life is," he says. O'Dell believes that the best job candidates not only will have clean cars—"no Slim-Fast cans or tennis balls rolling around in the backseat"—but will also excel at the casual conversation in a restaurant. "It's a way to learn the personal side of things—whether or not they have a family, whether they smoke, etc." that doesn't come out in the formal interview.

Dave Hall doesn't mind making candidates a little more nervous than they already are. Hall, a principal at Search Connection, likes to place want ads that list his company's name but not its phone number; he wants only candidates who'll bother to look the number up. When he's not entirely sure about candidates after their interviews, he instructs them to call him to follow up—and then doesn't return their first 3 calls. He says he's looking for employees who'll persist through a million no-thank-yous in making recruiting calls.

4. Do not run down former employers or coworkers. Prepare positive reasons for leaving any former position.

5. Show sincere interest in the company and the interviewer. Remember, your task is to sell yourself to the interviewer, not just to convince him or her that you are the best candidate for the position.

6. Know your résumé thoroughly. Be prepared to elaborate on part of it. The product you are selling is you. Know yourself.

Keep in mind that you are selling yourself in the interview process. Just as you would promote a product or service, you are now promoting yourself. Effective salespeople know their product, conduct research to determine their customer's needs, and use that knowledge to sell their product. During the interview the employer or company is the customer and you take on the role of the salesperson. Just as products do not sell themselves, neither do job candidates.

Note: Much of this may sound like an old-fashioned approach to interviewing—conservative dress, watching posture, not chewing gum, etc. Yes, it is! We are seeing a return to embracing these and other "traditional" values. Many companies are discontinuing "casual days" and are encouraging a more professional look. The casualness of recent years has backfired in lowering customer confidence. So in the interviewing process you can tip the scale in your favor by leaning toward the conservative side.

QUESTIONS ASKED BY THE INTERVIEWER

The following are some sample interview questions. Write out your answers to these questions; just thinking about them is not sufficient preparation for actually answering them. Writing out your answers will help you be more comfortable handling the same or similar questions in the interview. Remember, the interview is not just a formality since the interviewer has seen your great résumé; *the interview is the most important part of the whole process.* Here is where you have the opportunity to sell yourself. Prepare a 1- to 2-minute response to each question. If you take longer than that, the interviewer may feel you are trying to take control of the interview.

1. Tell me a little about yourself. _____

_____

_____

_____

2. What are your greatest strengths? What are 3 characteristics that would make you a good candidate for this position? _____

_____

_____

_____

3. What would your previous employer list as your greatest strengths? _____

_____

_____

_____

4. What motivates you to put forth your greatest effort? _____

_____

_____

_____

5. What have been some of your most significant accomplishments? How were you able to achieve those accomplishments? _____

_____

_____

_____

6. What have you done that has contributed to increased sales, profits, efficiency, etc.? _____

_____

_____

_____

7. What types of situations frustrate you? What are your weaknesses? What have you attempted and failed to accomplish? _____

_____

_____

_____

8. What are you looking for in a new position? Why do you want this job? What do you find attractive about this position? _____

_____

_____

_____

9. Why are you leaving your current job? _____

_____

_____

_____

10. What important changes or trends do you see in this industry? How do you think those changes will affect the way we succeed in this company? _____

_____

_____

_____

11. How long would it take you to make a meaningful contribution to our company? What are the areas where you would need more training? Do you feel you may be overqualified or too experienced for this position? _____

_____

_____

_____

12. What do you look for in a supervisor? Describe the relationship that should exist between a supervisor and his or her employee. What do you see as your most difficult task as a manager? What is your management style? _____

_____

_____

_____

13. Do you prefer working alone or as part of a team? Are you better working with things, people, or ideas? Are you better at creating or doing?_____

_____

_____

14. Describe an ideal working environment. In your last position, what were the things you liked most (least)? How do you handle pressure and deadlines? _____

_____

_____

_____

15. Where, on your list of priorities, does your job fall? What kind of things outside of work do you enjoy? What magazines do you like to read? Name 3 books you have read in the last year. Are you achieving personal goals you have set?_____

_____

_____

_____

16. Where would you like to be 5 years from now? What would you expect to be earning 5 years from now? Are you continuing your education? How are you staying current with changes in this industry? _____

_____

_____

_____

17. How long do you feel a person should stay in the same position? _____

_____

_____

_____

18. What does a typical weekend consist of for you? What do you do to relieve boredom?

_____

_____

_____

19. What other kinds of positions have you been looking at? If we do not select you for this position, would you be interested in another (office, sales, administrative, etc.) position within the company? How does this job compare with others for which you have interviewed? What makes this job different from your current/last one?_____

_____

_____

20. Why should we choose you for this position? What can you do for us that someone else cannot do? _____

_____

_____

_____

21. Do you have any questions? (A good interviewer will ask you this.)

Make sure you are ready with 4 or 5 questions. Even if the interviewer has answered everything you need to know, it will make you appear more interested and more knowledgeable if you ask a few questions.

Examples of questions to ask follow.

THE ONLY FIVE INTERVIEWING QUESTIONS THAT MATTER

I give lists of questions that interviewers may ask and that you should be prepared to answer. But along with "Why are manhole covers round?" Richard Bolles says there are really only 5 critical questions that employers are dying to know:

1. Why are you here?
2. What can you do for us?
3. What kind of person are you?
4. What distinguishes you from 19 other people who can do the same tasks that you can.
5. Can I afford you?

(Source: *What Color Is Your Parachute?* © 2004)

Keep in mind that any company is interested in hiring the whole person, not just your technical, administrative, computer, or sales (etc.) skills.

QUESTIONS TO ASK THE INTERVIEWER

In today's marketplace it is not enough to competently answer the interviewer's questions. You would be well advised to have prepared 4 to 5 questions to ask when given the opportunity. *People who ask questions appear brighter, more interested, and more knowledgeable.*

1. What would be a typical day's assignments?
2. What are the travel requirements, if any?
3. What is the typical career path in this position? What is a realistic time frame for advancement?
4. Where are the opportunities for greatest growth within the company?
5. What criteria are used to evaluate and promote employees here?
6. What type of training is available?
7. What kind of ongoing professional development programs are available to help me continue to grow?
8. Whom would I report to in this position? What can you tell me about that person's management style?
9. What management philosophy is used by the company?
10. How would you describe the company's culture (personality, environment)?
11. What is the company's mission statement? What are the company's goals?

12. What are the skills and attributes most needed to advance in this company?

13. Who will be this company's major competitors over the next 5 years? How will this company maintain an advantage over them?

14. What has been the growth pattern of this company over the last 5 years?

15. What do you see as upcoming changes in this industry?

16. Is this a new position, or would I be replacing someone?

17. What qualities are you looking for in the right person for this position?

18. Is there a written job description? May I see it?

19. How many people are in this department?

20. How do you see me complementing the existing group?

21. What do you enjoy about working for this company?

AFTER THE INTERVIEW

Few people receive offers after a first interview. Therefore, it is important that you initiate your own follow-up with the person with whom you interviewed. Your persistence and initiative may be the one small difference in making you the candidate of choice.

The follow-up letter. Nine out of 10 candidates still do not follow up on their interviews. The follow-up letter provides you with a great opportunity to once again put your name at the top of the candidate pool. The thank-you or follow-up letter is to express appreciation for the time of the interviewer and to confirm your interest in the position. It will also help the interviewer remember you clearly and demonstrate your professionalism and writing skills. Remember that with the introduction letter, cover letter and résumé, phone follow-up, interview, and now the follow-up letter, you have created 5 contact points with the person making the decision. Your name will be hard to forget.

Mention in the letter that you will keep in touch and indicate on what day you will make your first call. For example, "I will check back with you on Tuesday, August 23, to see if you require any additional information."

Maintain telephone contact for as long as there is a possibility that the position is still open. Decisions are frequently made slowly in any organization. Don't be too quick to assume you are not being considered. Your persistent follow-up may ultimately make you the candidate of choice.

It is imperative that you mail the follow-up letter no later than the next day following the interview.

Note: Continue to make follow-up contacts every 4 to 5 days following an interview until a decision has been made. Having invested your time in the interview, you have earned the right to know what decisions have been made.

Is it easy for you to describe your strongest areas of competence to someone else? Do you feel like you're bragging? _____

_____

_____

Are you aware of any personal habits or annoying filter words that may be part of your personal presentation? _____

_____

_____

Is your level of enthusiasm contagious?_____

_____

_____

_____

What red flags have you experienced in the past interview situations? Times when you recognized negative things in the opportunity being presented._____

_____

_____

_____

Chapter Ten

Negotiating Salaries

SHOW ME THE MONEY!

When the interviewing process is coming to an end, it's time to deal with the burning question, framed from both your perspective and that of the employer. You are thinking, *How much can I get here?* and the employer is thinking, *How much is this person going to cost me?*

Here are some principles to guide you:

1. Don't discuss salary until
   - you know exactly what the job requires,
   - they have decided they want you, and
   - you have decided you want them.

2. The responsibilities of the job determine the salary, not . . .
   - your education,
   - your experience, or
   - your previous salary.

3. To win at the salary negotiation, don't be the first one to bring it up. Instead:
   - Show genuine interest in what the job requires.
   - Don't ask about benefits, vacations, perks, etc. until you know you want the job.
   - If they ask too early what you need, simply respond, "Let's talk a little more about the posi tion to see if there's a match."

4. Recognize that many things can fall under the title of compensation:
   - a company car (preferably a BMW)
   - a country club or YMCA membership
   - free life insurance
   - medical plan
   - dental and vision plan
   - profit sharing
   - company stock
   - an expense account
   - tuition reimbursement

- additional time off
- relocation expenses
- your own laptop computer
- your own administrative assistant
- a free parking space
- unlimited M&Ms
- a sign-on bonus
- weekly massages
- two weeks in the company condo in Hawaii
- a Rolex watch after 90 days
- your birthday off
- a production bonus upon completion of a project
- educational opportunities for your children
- cell phone for business and personal use
- 401(k) contributions
- a low-interest loan for home purchase
- seminar attendance

You get the idea. Make this a fun process. I realize that negotiating anything is uncomfortable for some of you. If you don't enjoy going to Tijuana and bargaining for the turquoise necklace you want, you may be somewhat intimidated by this process. But realize that negotiating salary is not a confrontational process and certainly not a win/lose proposition.

Look at this scenario with me. Let's say Bob goes out to buy a car. He looks at a Ford Focus and decides that is what he wants. It's a basic model with no extras but seems to be a good buy on a dependable car to get him back and forth to school. Once he decides on the car, here are two possibilities:

 COMPANY PERKS—A BRAND NEW BMW?

Well, believe it or not, in today's desperate scramble for good employees, a BMW is not impossible. In fact, it's a reality at Revenue Systems Inc. in Alpharetta, Georgia. All 45 employees—from secretaries to managers—get to drive a brand new leased BMW at the company's expense. The company simply knew what their average recruiting costs were and put that money into the luxury car leases instead. The response from applicants—thousands of whom have sent in their resumes—would be enough to make other CEOs green with envy.

Ceil Diaz left her job working for the state of Illinois to join a Chicago ad firm. There, she receives a basket of flowers and gift certificates on her 1-year job anniversary and got to meet with architects to help plan her work space.

John Nuveen & Co., a Chicago investment bank, pays the bulk of college tuition for the children of employees who have been with the company for at least 5 years. How would you like to have someone to walk your dog? What about an errand runner to pick up groceries for your family? Built in day care and on-site $3.00 haircuts?

Starting to make that annual Thanksgiving turkey look a little slim, huh?

1. An inexperienced salesperson will breathe a sigh of relief and lead Bob into the finance and insurance office before he changes his mind. He will take his little commission and go on to the next buyer.

2. Here is what a mature, experienced salesperson would do. He would continue talking to Bob. He would ask if he has a favorite kind of music. Of course he does. "Wouldn't it be nice to have a great sound system in this car?" the salesman asks. "With spring just around the corner, you know how much you would enjoy a sunroof?" Since you are in school, it will be important to make this car last for a long time. It would be advisable to have fabric protection, undercoating, and rust-proofing applied. For those long trips back home to family, wouldn't it be nice to have cruise control? And so on. Ultimately, Bob walks out, a happy customer, but with a payment of $100 a month more than he had originally planned. Has he been tricked? Of course not. He has simply been shown the benefits of some things he really did want. Once the company has made its initial decision to hire you, you can freely discuss additional benefits and compensation with little fear of changing the company's basic decision that it wants you!

Have you ever negotiated your salary or compensation package? Or have you always assumed it was "take it or leave it"? _____

_____

_____

_____

What are you doing in the salary-negotiating process? Keep in mind, if you have handled the interview as described, salary did not come up until you decided you wanted the job, and more importantly, the hiring manager wants you. At that point, and not until that point, you are in a position to negotiate. Also, keep in mind that if you have done an effective job search, you should be talking with more than 1 company anyway. On the next page is an illustration that shows the timing for discussing salary.

"THE TIMES, THEY ARE A'CHANGIN"

Change we can count on, but that doesn't mean opportunities are decreasing. True, not all change is progress, but all progress does require change. Embrace the change by positioning yourself for new options.

I recently worked with a young woman who had lost her job, making in the mid-70s. Panicked and convinced she could never find another job in that income range, she had decided she would have to start her own business. However, after identifying her unique areas of competence, I advised against that and encouraged her to do a creative job search. In a short period of time she had two offers on the table; the clearly better fit had offered her a base salary of $89,000. We discussed the offer, the fact that it was a great fit, and she went back and asked for $98,000. They settled at a base of $94,000 with some additional benefits bringing her package to approximately $105,000.

Now this is in a market where "no one is hiring," we are in a "recession," and unemployment is increasing. Be careful of the generalities. All you need is one right opportunity. The sky is not falling. Economists and naysayers will always be pessimistic about the future. Remember, the best way to predict your future is to create it.

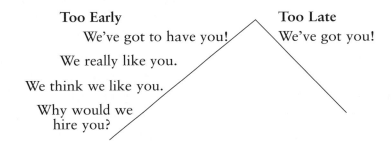

Too Early

We've got to have you!

We really like you.

We think we like you.

Why would we
hire you?

Too Late

We've got you!

At this point, you should be prepared. You should know what comparable salaries are for this position. That and the responsibilities of the position determine what your compensation should be. A couple of years ago, I worked with a young woman who had been fired from a position in which she made $19,000 per year for clerical work. She decided that's not what she wanted to do anyway and began to get focused on what she did want. It was somewhat of a redirection, but she was enthusiastic and confident. After having done an excellent job search, she began interviewing for positions in graphic design and marketing. She interviewed for a position advertised at $32,500. She came out of that interview with a salary package of $54,000. The company does not know to this day that in her last job she was making $19,000, nor does it need to know. That has nothing to do with what she is being paid now. She relayed the benefits of what she had to offer and was compensated based on the value of that.

Always focus on the job you are going to, not where you are coming from. There is no law that says your pay will increase by only 4 percent a year or even 10 percent. The world is a giving place, and if you can convey your benefits, the world will give you what you are worth. We have had many clients who have increased their compensation dramatically because they learned to focus on what they were going to rather than looking at what they just came from.

Also, recognize that your *needs* are *not* the determinant of how you are paid. If you apply at Taco Bell, it is irrelevant whether you have a $1,200 per month house payment and a $450 per month car note; Taco Bell is not going to pay you $40,000 per year. Your needs are not the company's concern. I recently had a young woman come into my office in distress. She had gone in to her boss that morning and explained that she had just moved into a nicer apartment and purchased a new car and could no longer manage on what they were paying her. They fired her on the spot. I laughed when she told me this story. I totally agreed with the company. What she did to obligate herself to higher payments had nothing to do with how she should be paid.

Be sure you know your value and then market yourself in that range. In my experience, I find that people often give themselves about a $10,000 window from which to work. If they have been making $30,000, they will look at positions that pay about $25,000 to $35,000. But if they see a perfectly matched position paying $65,000, they don't bother to apply. Be careful of setting your own limitations. You will end up pretty much where you expect to end up.

Keep these principles in mind:

1. You must make the company money. As a rule of thumb, you must make the company 3 to 5 times your salary for hiring you to make sense.

2. Your compensation almost always relates to your level of responsibility. If it's easy to replace you, you aren't worth a whole lot.

3. Your work is an intangible. Few salaries are written in concrete. Companies that budget $38,000 for a position will start out trying to hire someone for $31,000. Recognize that the first offer is probably not what the company has in the budget.

4. Once you agree on a package, get it in writing. If you have been creative in this process, it is necessary to write out what you verbally agreed on. Don't have to defend later what you thought was said.

Have fun in the process. Don't say yes until everything matches your goals. In times of low unemployment, you are in the driver's seat.

Do you know what you're really worth? Have you checked sites like www.salary.com for comparable pay ranges? _____

_____

_____

_____

Can you see how in changing companies you may be able to double your income? Once you know your true value, you may realize you have been underemployed in your current or last position. Does the idea of marketing yourself with a clear understanding of your value excite you? Or does this whole process sound too much like buying a used car from the guy down on the corner?

_____

_____

_____

TAKEAWAYS

1. I need to see this as a selling process. I am selling a product, and that product is me.
2. I'm not too young, too old, or too short. I have unique areas of competence that could be of value to many companies.
3. I am in the driver's seat in this process. I don't have to beg for a job; rather I will choose from several offers.
4. I can bypass even people with more education or work experience because I know how to do an effective job search.

REFLECTIONS ON THIS SECTION

1. Review résumé myths. Ask yourself those questions and think about any new insight it adds to what you thought previously.
2. Consider the different résumé formats shown in this section. The right format and the right information are always determined by where you want to go. Don't have things on a resume that do not strengthen a focused presentation.
3. Review the job-search strategy section. Understanding this process can break even long periods of inability to get jobs. It must be done as written. If you send out well-constructed résumé and cover letters only, it can still require more than two hundred to get a job offer.
4. Review interviewing skills. These are the essential elements to learn.
5. Focus on the importance of having some questions to ask in the interview.

6. Get excited as you review the negotiating salaries section. This can change significantly what you accomplish in the financial area of your life, even if your work path remains the same.

IMMEDIATE ASSIGNMENTS

1. Begin a list of target companies.
2. Prepare an introduction letter and a cover letter.
3. Thoroughly understand the job search strategy section.
4. Listen to the second half of CD 2.

48 DAYS
Hall of Fame

Bennet was excited that Dell Computers was coming to town. Surely this was his chance to move up. After 7 years at a major university as a computer specialist, he was ready to get into a more progressive, innovative environment. Furthermore, he was confident his skills could be put to better use. In addition, he was hopeful that he could increase his $36,000 salary to perhaps even $45,000.

Knowing we cannot control the hiring process of any one company, I encouraged Bennet to broaden his list of target companies to at least twenty, rather than just one. I assured him this would increase his options and give us a truer picture of his marketability. He reluctantly agreed and began his job search.

Having a specific set of computer skills in a lesser used computer language proved to be very interesting to prospective employers. Although Bennet never even got an interview with Dell, he did in fact get several interviews with other companies. With the interest of multiple companies, he discovered the power of being able to negotiate salary. The offer he accepted was as follows: Base Salary—$120,000. Company Stock—12,000 shares currently valued at $10 per share (another $120,000). Sign-On Bonus—$15,000. Bennet more than quadrupled his income because he learned how to do a proper job search and how to negotiate.

Be careful of setting limitations that aren't really there!

(See www.48Days.com.)

Section V

Nontraditional Work

- Welcome to the last, but important, section.
- There are a lot of options for this session.
- By now you have started refining your résumé, identifying your target companies, and begun your initial contacts.
- We have found, however, that about half of the people who come to this stage of the process realize they really would like to do something on their own. They are tired of feeling victimized by downsizing and outsourcing, and are ready to take more control of their time and income.
- Thus this session can address some of the changes and opportunities.
1. In today's work environment we have a lot of choices. Sometimes the best options are only a subtle change from what you have been doing.

2. If you focus on results rather than on time, you will open up all kinds of new opportunities.

3. You don't have to change who you are, even if you want to do something on your own or start your own business. In the same way that we integrate skills and abilities, personality traits, and values, dreams, and passions in a traditional job, we also integrate those characteristics in a creative or nontraditional choice.

Chapter Eleven

Maybe I Don't Want a Traditional Job!

DO YOU HAVE WHAT IT TAKES?

Do you have what it takes to do something on your own?

In working with people over the years, we have identified a number of traits that indicate if people are likely to become successful in their own business. The more yes answers you have to the questions below, the more likely you have what it takes to run your own business. Each of the 18 questions is followed by a statement of why that particular trait is important.

_____**1. Are you a self-starter?** Successful business owners are always making things happen. They don't wait around for the phone to ring or to be told what to do next.

_____**2. Do you get along with different kinds of people?** Every business, even small ones, requires contact with a variety of people: customers, suppliers, bankers, and printers.

_____**3. Do you have a positive outlook?** Optimism and a sense of humor are critical factors for success. You have to be able to view setbacks and small failures as stepping-stones to your eventual success.

_____**4. Are you able to make decisions?** It has been said that indecision is the greatest thief of opportunity. Procrastination is the main obstacle to good decision-making. In a successful business important decisions are made on a daily basis, not put off. Eighty percent of decisions should be made right away.

_____**5. Are you able to accept responsibility?** If you typically blame others, the company, the government, or your spouse for what goes wrong, you are probably a poor candidate for running your own business. Successful business owners accept responsibility for results even if those results are not favorable.

_____**6. Do you enjoy competition?** You don't have to be cutthroat, but you must enjoy the thrill of competition. You must have a strong desire to compete, even against your own accomplishments of yesterday.

_____7. **Do you have willpower and self-discipline?** Self-discipline is the one key characteristic that makes all these others work. Without it you will not succeed.

_____8. **Do you plan ahead?** Every successful businessperson develops a long-term perspective. Going into business with a detailed plan dramatically increases the likelihood of business success. If you are already a goal-setter, you are more likely to succeed on your own.

_____9. **Can you take advice from others?** Being in your own business does not mean you have all the answers. Being open to the wisdom and experience of others is the hallmark of a leader. People who are willing to listen, spend more time doing what works the first time, rather than having to experience every mistake are more likely to succeed.

_____10. **Are you adaptable to changing conditions?** Change is constant in today's marketplace. Experts estimate that 80 percent of all products and services we are using today will be obsolete in 5 years. In every change there are the seeds of opportunity, thus successful people view change as an opportunity, not as a threat.

_____11. **Can you stick with it?** Most new ventures do not take off as quickly as we would like. Are you prepared to make at least a 1-year commitment to this business no matter how bleak it may look at times? Will you continue even if your friends tell you to throw in the towel?

_____12. **Do you have a high level of confidence and belief in what you are doing?** This is no time for doubt or second thoughts. You must absolutely believe in what you are doing. If you don't have total belief, you will not be able to sell the idea, product, or service to investors or customers. Don't deceive yourself into thinking that you can do well something you don't really believe in.

_____13. **Do you enjoy what you are going to do?** Don't ever think you can be successful doing something just for the money rewards. Ultimately, you must get a sense of meaning and satisfaction from what you are doing. So only consider those ideas about which you are totally passionate.

_____14. **Can you sell yourself and your ideas?** Many people fail with a great product or service because no one is out selling. Nobody will beat a path to your door even if you do have a better mousetrap. Those days are gone. You will need to sell constantly.

_____15. **Are you prepared to work long hours?** Few businesses are immediately successful. Most require months or years of long hours to get them going. It's like getting a plane off the ground. A great deal of energy is required at first, but once you are in the air, it takes less energy to keep moving. Businesses are much the same.

_____16. **Do you have the physical and emotional energy to run a business?** Operating your own business can be more draining than working for someone else because now you have to make all the decisions and probably do all the work initially.

_____17. **Do you have the support of your family and/or spouse?** Without support at home, your chances of success are dramatically reduced. Doubt and misgivings can too easily creep in. The less support you have, the more you will feel yourself being pushed back to being a traditional employee.

_____18. **Are you willing to risk your money in this venture?** If you are not, you probably question your confidence in the venture and your commitment to it. No bank or outside lender will be willing to take risk that you are not willing to back with everything you have.

More and more Americans are looking for greater control of their destinies and for the freedom that having your own business allows. One key to success is to make sure you match your personal skills with the proper business choice. Your work must integrate your skills, your personality tendencies, and your interests. That may seem simple and obvious, but it is amazing how often those simple principles are violated. The more you know and understand about yourself and match that up with your business direction, the more you exponentially increase your chances for success.

The downsizing of corporate America and the accompanying insecurity have fueled a resurgence of what we call "nontraditional" work. These factors have also prompted the concept of having a core career, in which a person has a job that keeps a roof overhead and food on the table but also has 1 or 2 other profit-producing ideas in place as well. With the exploding opportunities in home-based businesses, many Americans are finding that it makes more sense to use this model than to attempt to find that one right job that provides all their needs.

You may not see yourself as a typical entrepreneur or business owner. But in going through any transition you must recognize all the options for selecting work. It would be shortsighted only to look for a traditional job when that model is in fact diminishing. Just be aware of the new work models and ways to apply your unique skills.

Currently, about 60 percent of American homes have a business operating within their walls. Based on current trends, that number will grow to 72 percent in the next 5 years. This does not mean that the home-based business provides all the income for that family. It also does not mean that this is just someone selling a little soap and bringing in an extra $100 a month. The average home-based business in 2003 generated a little over $52,000.

Brian Tracy, a nationally known sales and business consultant, says most of us have 3 or 4 ideas a year that would make us millionaires if we just did something with those ideas. But most dismiss the ideas as impractical, unrealistic, or too expensive, or we think that someone probably already tried it. Thus we lose the opportunity to change our own success.

What are 3 or 4 ideas you have had over the years that you have on the back burner or have since seen someone else develop? _____

_____

_____

_____

What product or service idea do you have now? _____

_____

_____

Opportunities in service businesses, telecommunications, computer and Internet options, and network marketing all provide some explosive new choices. Many of these erase the old requirements of just exchanging time for dollars. You may be accustomed to receiving $10 an hour or $37,000 a year as an exchange of *time* and *effort*. But how do you relate to the idea of using an Internet site to provide information and see the potential of bringing in $1,000 a day? Or what about a mail-order product for your gardening interest that produces hundreds of orders weekly, so that you are being compensated for *results*, not time and effort?

Be aware of this change from a time-and-effort economy to a results-based economy. If you went into a buggy shop in 1896 and ordered a small wagon, you would not have guaranteed that craftsman $10 an hour or agreed that he would receive $37,000 annually. Rather, you would have agreed on a set price for the finished product—let's say $100 for a finished wagon. Now, whether it took that craftsman 15 hours or 200 hours was not your concern; you simply paid for the completed wagon. This is a model based on results, not time and effort. What we are seeing in our current work environment is a return to that simple model. Even companies are beginning to say, "We will not guarantee payment just because you showed up for work; rather we will compensate you based on the production completed." A recent contract at Saturn in Spring hill, Tennessee, included this concept. The employees there are being paid an agreed-upon base pay but receive their real bonuses based on the profitability of the company. This is a healthy return to a realistic method of compensation.

Describe 3 or 4 times in your own work experience when you have been paid on results or on completion of the job rather than just for putting in your time.

It may be necessary or advantageous for you to consider the unusual or unique as you explore new work opportunities. If you think of a teacher, you may immediately visualize a city schoolroom with thirty-two kids in the classroom. But you could also be a teacher working for IBM and living in London, England. You could work for a sign company and be paid $15 an hour. But would you be willing to work for that same sign company and be paid $6 for every real estate sign you could paint this week? Or what about mowing yards at $65 each? Or advertising a family recipe in the back of a cooking magazine where you receive $3 for each order? If you are willing to look at new models, it will greatly expand the opportunities for you.

A recent client, though he has advanced academic degrees, greatly enjoys the challenges of removing moles from people's yards. We are now developing a prototype for that business, which has all the possibilities of growing into a successfully franchised business. Watch for *The Molenator!*

For a more comprehensive overview of nontraditional opportunities, order the *48 Days to Creative Income* workbook and audio. Available from 48 Days: www.48days.com/products.php#creative_income.

For free articles on nontraditional work and to subscribe to a free weekly newsletter, go to www.48Days.com.

Some ideas for successful nontraditional businesses are:

1. Franchises: The hottest form of new business. For a franchise fee, you can purchase a proven concept for your business. Success rates are high. You typically pay a percentage of all revenues as a franchise "royalty." Franchises range from expensive ($500,000) to inexpensive ($1,200). (Check out the options at www.franchise.com or www.franchisehandbook.com/index.asp.)

2. Business Opportunities: Another form of purchasing a concept. It is not as heavily regulated as franchises, so do enough checking to feel comfortable with your choice. Here is a helpful site: www.busop1.com.

3. Licensing: You can sell NASCAR T-shirts or Tiger Woods golf clubs, but you will need to pay a licensing fee for using a well-known name.

4. Distributorships: These are usually received just by asking the manufacturer or publishing company. For example, I am a distributor for several publishing companies, where I purchase their book titles at 50 percent discount.

5. Home-Based Businesses: You may purchase a small initial inventory and be provided a little training, but for the most part you are just buying an idea, and you are on your own. The positives are that the cost is usually low and you have no ongoing fees to the company that you purchased from. See an example at www.smcorp.com.

And here are some more ideas for things you can do on your own:

Accounting	Wedding Planning
eBay Sales	Real Estate
Personal Service	Senior Citizen Care
Portrait Painting	Wedding Photography
Graphic Design	Computer Consultant
Gift Baskets	Newsletters
Vending	Delivery Service
Interior Decorating	Flea Market Vendor
Landscape Design	Home Inspection
Ceiling Fans	Import/Export Broker
House Painting	Auto Detailing
Consignment Used Cars	Glass Tinting
Child Security Systems	Power Washing
Nutrition Counselor	Wild Herbs
One-Person Entertainer	Catering
Organic Gardening	Tour Guide
Tree Removal	Chimney Cleaning
Decks and Coverings	Scholarship Search
Homeschooling Counselor	Manners Instruction
Mail Order	Balloon Vendor
Pet Sitter	Real Estate Photos
Aerial Photos	Discount Coupon Books
Internet Marketing	How-to Brochures

Add your own ideas to this list. Search the back classified ads in magazines like *Entrepreneur, Business Start-Ups, Income Opportunities,* and more.

FREQUENTLY ASKED BUSINESS START-UP QUESTIONS

1. What are the key ingredients for success?

The ability to plan, organize, and communicate. And remember, 85 percent of your success will originate from your people skills—attitude, enthusiasm, self-discipline—and only 15 percent will be due to your technical skills.

2. Don't most new businesses fail?

Once upon a time, someone churned out the statistic that 4 out of 5 small businesses fail in their first 5 years of operation. No one can trace the source of this mysterious figure. It is not only illogical but also totally untrue. According to a Dun & Bradstreet census of 250,000 businesses, almost 70 percent of all firms that start in any given year are still around in some form 10 years later. The study pinpointed the true failure rate at less than 1 percent of all businesses per year.

Here's what often happens. George starts a lawn mowing service. Two years later he recognizes that George's Yard Service has a lot of competitors. But he also recognized that 70 percent of his customers are candidates for a waterfall in their yard. He changes his business to George's Waterworks to take advantage of the new opportunity. Statistics will show that his first business is no longer around and therefore must have failed. But he didn't fail; he simply moved on to another business. That's a common path for people who start businesses.

3. Will we really see more and more small businesses?

Many of you have already experienced the downsizing of large corporations. IBM, General Motors, and other American standards have cut their workforces dramatically. A recent article in *Time* announced an average of 1,963 job losses each day in America. The good news is that since 1982 alone, the number of small businesses has grown by 50 percent, to approximately 24.5 million. In the last 10 years, small business has accounted for 71 percent of the nation's new job growth, now adding over 2 million new jobs each year. Small businesses employ 54 percent of the American workforce. What we are seeing is a healthy return to the kind of business that our country was founded on.

4. Are there any new ideas left to start?

Experts estimate that more than 85 percent of the products and services we use today will be obsolete in 5 years. The airplane, tape recorder, artificial heart valve, soft contact lens, and personal computer were all new ideas in past years. With the changes we are experiencing in today's market, there are thousands of opportunities for new ideas.

5. What if I'm not creative?

You don't have to be original to be successful in business. If you can do something 10 percent better than it is currently being done or provide added value, you can be wildly successful. When Domino's got into the pizza business, it did not make better or cheaper pizza; it simply added delivery to a very common product. Meeting the desire for speed and convenience, Domino's created millionaires all across the country.

6. If I share my idea, will someone steal it?

Ideas are a dime a dozen. It's not even the quality of the idea but rather the quality of the action plan brought to that idea that determines success. Share your idea with others and get their input. Try your idea on friends and family. Make one prototype and see if people will buy it. Then gear up for a business supporting that idea.

7. Should I buy a franchise, distributorship, or business opportunity?

The attraction of these options is that they are a tried system for a business concept. Normally, that means a proven track to run on, marketing support, and name recognition. But buyer beware: make sure you research carefully, so you don't overpay for something you could do yourself.

After considering these options, you are ready to create your own 48-day plan! Check out chapter 12 for additional help but then begin to work through the stages of your individual plan. You can do this. You can achieve the success you are seeking. Take inventory, focus, create a plan and act.

48 DAYS
Hall of Fame

Fredrico and Sallie Consuego were newcomers to the United States. Fredrico had been making a successful living as a sales representative but was frustrated by the lack of fulfillment in just doing a job well. In clarifying long term direction and goals, it became clear that his passion was to someday have a coffee house, full of the aromas, sights and sounds of his native Italy. While considering this to be a long range, future goal, he and Sallie sought career counseling and were challenged to pursue their dream now, being encouraged to believe that a clear plan and passion precede money and fulfillment. Although concerned about the lack of business experience and financial strength, Fredrico and Sallie eagerly began exploring possibilities.

Established franchises for coffee houses estimated that between $180,000 and $220,000 was required to successfully begin this type of business. Fredrico and Sallie were told to refine their ideas, the look, the menu, the hours, and the name. As their excitement grew, their belief grew as well.

Ninety days later, Caffe Italiano opened. The tables and chairs were purchased from a salvage company and had been splash painted with a contemporary design. The carpet had been pulled up and another unique paint treatment had been applied to the floor. One of Fredrico's friends had built the serving counter for $550. The neon sign in the window proudly displayed Caffe Italiano. The espresso machine was in place and an initial inventory of coffee beans was available. The total cost leading to opening day was less than $8,000. A few well-placed news items were picked up by the major newspapers and led to immediate standing-room only evening performances.

Three years later, Caffe Italiano has moved to a new $1,000,000 prime location, featuring 8 shows weekly. Their success and ambiance attracted several major investors, allowing Fredrico to grow beyond his wildest dreams and entertain requests for new locations in cities all across the nation.

Although Italian by birth, Fredrico and Sallie prove once again that they are AmeriCANS, not AmeriCANTS.

(See www.48Days.com.)

Chapter Twelve

Final Components for Making the Plan!

EIGHT REASONS WHY YOU ARE NOT GETTING A JOB OFFER!

Are you really too old, too young, overqualified, or lacking the right education? Is the deck really stacked against you? Not likely! Chances are you only need to improve the way you present yourself.

Recently, a woman approached me after one of our seminar presentations on career management. She had been through 63 job interviews and wanted me to look at her résumé to see what was preventing her from getting job offers. Hearing that she had 63 interviews let me know I did not need to look at her résumé at all; it was doing an excellent job since getting interviews is the only purpose of a résumé. So her problem was not in the résumé but something in her personal presentation.

Here are the 8 reasons most commonly given by human resource people give for rejecting people:

1. Lack of Enthusiam

You don't have to be a Zig Ziglar or a David Letterman, but you must express enthusiasm for a job if you don't want to be weeded out immediately. Enthusiasm, boldness, and confidence will often do more for you in an interview than another college degree.

2. Lack of Interpersonal Skills

When a candidate even hints at an inability to get along with others, it dramatically weakens that person's chances in an interview. While this sounds obvious, it's surprising how open some people are about their faults. Someone who interrupts frequently will not be seen as a good team player.

3. What's in It for Me?

We know you want to know about benefits, vacations, etc., but don't lead with these questions. First, the employer will want to know what you can do for the company. You can't negotiate for more vacation time before you've been offered a job. Convince the employer that you are the right person for the job, be sure that you want to work there, then you can discuss pay and benefits.

4. Unclear Job Goals

Don't be a generalist. Be clear about the job you are seeking. If the interviewer gets the impression that you are just looking for a job rather than a specific opportunity to use your skills, you will sabotage your chances.

5. Poor Personal Appearance

The key here is to fit in with the organization you are contacting. I will defend your right to wear cutoffs and a baseball cap, but if you really want a job, you must dress appropriately. Many times I hear people who are irritated about not being given a job when they have a nose ring, bad breath, and unshined shoes. Keep in mind that organizations hire people, not credentials and experience. If they don't like you, it doesn't matter how great your experience is—you won't get the job.

6. Unprepared for the Interview

If you fumble when asked basic questions, you will appear unprepared and uncaring about the process. When asked, "Tell me a little about yourself" you should have a concise 2-minute answer; 15 seconds about your personal background, 1.5 minutes about your work experience, and 15 seconds about what you can do for this company. The time you spent preparing for the interview will be time invested wisely.

7. Not Being Clear on Your Strengths

You should be able to state without hesitation 3 characteristics that would make you a great candidate for any given job you are applying for. If you cannot clearly identify your strengths, no interviewer will attempt to convince you what they are.

8. Not Selling Yourself

Even if you would not enjoy selling vacuum cleaners door-to-door, you have to realize that in the interview process, you are selling yourself. Especially in today's market, you have to promote yourself. Follow up immediately with a thank-you note and with a telephone call 3 or 4 days later. It's a good way to reinforce your interest in the job as well as ask a question or 2 you may have forgotten in the interview.

Today's workplace is desperately seeking competent workers. Know how you are gifted, present yourself with confidence, follow up, and be ready to have multiple offers from which to choose.

PERSONAL MISSION STATEMENT WORKSHEET

This can be a powerful process. We have heard a lot in the last few years about companies creating a mission statement. That statement will define their focus, and every activity in that organization should line up with and embrace that mission statement. You can do the same thing as an individual, and the power of having a clear focus will likely surprise you.

Drawing from the information you have already completed, fill in this simple worksheet. Look at the examples on the next page and just get something down for yourself. You can come back to it and refine it over time, but there is real power in having something to help you focus what your life is really all about. This is a concept that has been popularized in the last few years. If you can get something down on paper, it will separate you from about 98 percent of the people on the face of the earth. Just get something down; then you can come back to it periodically to update and revise it.

This is just a summary of the components you have been developing throughout the workbook. Now put them down and integrate them into your own Personal Mission Statement. (Some examples follow on the next couple pages.)

Skills and Interests: _____

_____

_____

_____

Personality Traits: _____

_____

_____

_____

_____

Values, Dreams, and Passions:_____

_____

_____

_____

_____

My Mission:_____

_____

_____

_____

For a more complete mission statement planning form, e-mail Dan at mission@48Days.com, simply putting mission in the subject line. You will receive a more extensive personal mission statement planning worksheet immediately. Yes, it's free!

"God has given each of you some special abilities; be sure to use
them to help each other, passing on to others God's many kinds of
blessings." (1 Pet. 4:10 TLB)

EXAMPLES OF MISSION STATEMENTS

I will maintain a positive attitude and a sense of humor in everything I do. I want to be known by my family as a caring and loving husband and father, by my business associates as a fair and honest person, and by my friends as someone they can count on. To the people who work for me and with me, I pledge my respect, and I will strive every day to earn their respect. Controlling all my actions is a strong sense of integrity that I believe to be my most important character trait.

My mission is to provide service, products, and benefits with integrity and honesty to the medical community. I will look for opportunities to help hurting individuals and assist other professionals in a win-win manner. I will not knowingly harm or take advantage of anyone. I will use my knowledge and abilities in organizing and structuring in ways that provide income and pleasure for my family and blessings to those around me.

My mission is to exercise my creativity and innovative ideas by developing songs, books, and products that change lives and society for the better. I will use my talents and abilities consistently. I will not hide them simply because they will not always be immediately recognized. I want all of my work to be a product of God's inspiration and a blessing to the world. I will be loyal to family, friends, and God.

For myself, I want to develop self-knowledge, self-love and self-allowing. I want to use my healing talents to keep hope alive and express my vision courageously in word and action. In my family I want to build healthy, loving relationships in which we let one another become our best selves. At work I want to establish a fault-free, self-perpetuating learning environment. In the world, I want to nurture the development of all life forms in harmony with the laws of nature.

My mission is to use my skills and experience in design to help people realize their dreams for their homes and themselves. In order to do this with increasing effectiveness, I will study and expand my own knowledge in God's word, design, finance, sales, and social skills. I will strive for loving relationships with my immediate and extended family and many friends. I will invest love, service, time, patience, encouragement, and creativity into those relationships. I will listen more than I talk and be transparent in sharing personal insights and struggle. From now on I will strive for excellence in all of the above and in my hobby of music.

Appendix

SUGGESTED READING LIST

Allen, Robert. *Multiple Streams of Income*. A masterful guide to insulating yourself against corporate decisions by developing multiple streams of income, using real estate, investing, and the Internet.

Allen, Robert. *Multiple Streams of Internet Income*. How ordinary people make extraordinary money online. I use this with clients when we are working with an Internet site as part of their business.

Andrews, Andy. *The Traveler's Gift*. A delighted little book in which the writer tells a story of a dream traveler who meets 7 important people from history. From each one he learns an important life principle.

Bolles, Richard Nelson. *What Color Is Your Parachute? A Practical Manual for Job-Hunters and Career-Changers*. The best single source for the career process. Updated every year. Many practical tips and processes for guiding through the search.

Bolles, Richard Nelson. *Where Do I Go from Here with My Life?* A practical and effective life/work planning manual for all ages.

Boldt, Laurence G. *Zen and the Art of Making a Living*. Another artistic way to look at the life you want and then develop your career around that.

Buford, Bob. *Halftime*. This book takes a Christian look at the change in life where we become more interested in significance than success.

Cameron, Julia. *The Artist's Way*. A delightful guide to rediscovering your creativity and authentic self. Julia shows how we are all artistic and creative. We may need to rediscover those qualities.

Carnegie, Dale. *How to Stop Worrying and Start Living*. Based on the premise, "What's the worst that could happen?" this book teaches you to build from there. If you've had a disaster in your life, this book can encourage you to look at where you are and move forward.

Carnegie, Dale. *How to Win Friends and Influence People*. Old-time favorite about how to treat people and gain positive influence.

Covey, Stephen R. *First Things First*. Expansion of one of the *7 Habits* books, shows how to set clear priorities in your life.

Covey, Stephen R. *The 7 Habits of Highly Effective People.* Dynamic presentation of how to develop direction and a personal mission statement. It's rather textbookish, but don't get bogged down in the details; just understand the principles.

Covey, Stephen R. *The 8th Habit—from Effectiveness to Greatness.* Another bulky 410-page book to tell you a simple principle: "Find your own voice and help others find theirs." If you're using the 48 Days principles, you're already doing this.

Edwards, Paul and Sarah. *Making It on Your Own.* How to change your thinking from employee to working for yourself. In today's work environment, you need to be willing to look at new work models.

Edwards, Paul and Sarah. *Working From Home.* Everything you need to know about living and working under the same roof. Updated every couple of years so you will find current information. Check their Web site for all current books. Their information is up-to-date, accurate, and extremely helpful: www.homeworks.com.

Eikleberry, Carol. *The Career Guide for Creative and Unconventional People.* A wonderful guide for applying your artistic, writing, musical, or other creative skills in ways that can make you money.

Frankl, Viktor E. *Man's Search for Meaning.* A classic work by a concentration camp prisoner, who identifies that even when everything else is taken away, we have the ability to choose. (I read this one about every six months just to remind myself of what is really important.)

Gire, Ken. *Windows of the Soul.* One of my favorite books ever. A gentle guide to help us see God in new ways. I believe it opens our eyes to see more opportunities all around us in the process. A timeless classic.

Guiness, Os. *The Call.* A critical-thinking book about how to find God's central purpose for your life.

Hanson, Mark Victor and Robert G. Allen. *The One Minute Millionaire.* Presenting the enlightened way to wealth—not at the expense of others but by helping others in the process. A must-read.

Hill, Napoleon. *Think and Grow Rich.* One of the greatest best-sellers of all time about how to think yourself into a new way of living.

Johnson, Spencer. *The Present.* A quick read that shows the importance of learning from the past, planning for the future, but living in the present.

Johnson, Spencer. *Who Moved My Cheese?* A modern allegory about changing work environments. Don't expect things to always be the same. If you are not prepared, you will feel like a victim.

Jones, Laurie Beth. *The Path.* A great resource for creating your mission statement for work and for life. Whereas *7 Habits of Highly Successful People* will tell you the importance of a mission statement, *The Path* will show you how to do it.

Kiyosaki, Robert. *Rich Dad, Poor Dad.* This book may open your eyes to see how to be successful in work and business. It dispels a lot of American myths about how to be successful.

Lee, Blaine. *The Power Principle.* Another great book from Covey Leadership Center. Living by the principles outlined in this book will do more for your true success than having a marketing strategy for a new product.

Levinson, Jay Conrad. *The Guerrilla Marketing Handbook.* Great tips for marketing yourself or your small business. Jay has several books on guerilla marketing that are all useful and practical for low-cost ways to build your business. Check out all the guerilla marketing titles at www.gmar keting.com/books/books.html.

Mackay, Harvey. *We Got Fired*. Harvey interviewed 28 famous people who have experienced being fired at least once. The list includes the former head of the American Red Cross, the founder of The Home Depot, a Super Bowl coach, and the chief executive of Bank One. Read how being fired is compared to being kicked with a "golden horseshoe."

McAlindon, Harold. *The Little Book of Big Ideas*. Chock-full of tips on releasing your creative thinking and seeing opportunities all around and contains wonderful quotations from the world's most creative minds.

Pink, Daniel. *Free Agent Nation*. Does a great job of describing the changing model of "employee" to "free agent."

Quindlen, Anna. *A Short Guide to a Happy Life*. What does it take to live deeply and success-fully rather than just to exist? This little book puts in perspective those things we often consider to be too important.

Ramsey, Dave. *Financial Peace*. The best all-around source for getting your finances in order. This *New York Times* best-seller has transformed the finances of thousands.

Ramsey, Dave. *The Total Money Makeover*. This is a proven plan for financial fitness. Thousands of people have become debt-free and are running their lives and businesses with no debt. This book tells you how you can do it too.

Schwartz, David. *The Magic of Thinking Big*. Workable methods for thinking big. How to create your own "good luck." The book that put coach Lou Holtz on the road to extraordinary success.

Shenson, Howard. *Shenson on Consulting*. The best overview of making the transition from a regular job to consulting.

Sinetar, Marsha. *To Build the Life You Want, Create the Work You Love*. An excellent guide to looking at your life and building priorities around values. Marsha is a delightful writer who will challenge your thinking and convince you that doing what you love is possible.

Stanley, Thomas J. *The Millionaire Mind*. A phenomenal follow-up to *The Millionaire Next Door*. This one tells the top common characteristics of truly wealthy people. They might surprise you.

Stanley, Thomas J. *The Millionaire Next Door*. An excellent overview of wealth-building principles.

Weiss, Andrew. *Million Dollar Consulting*. A textbook manual on becoming a high-level consultant.

Wiseman, Richard. *The Luck Factor*. Luck is not something that just happens to some people. We create our own luck. Want to dramatically increase yours? Read this.

Zelinski, Ernie J. *The Joy of Not Working*. A humorous look at the benefits of not working.

Ziglar, Zig. *See You at the Top*. Long-time favorite about positive thinking and winning atti-tudes. One of my personal favorites for children, teenagers, and adults.

AUDIO PROGRAMS

Tapes and CDs are a powerful method of getting new information and increasing your ability to go to new levels of accomplishment. If you travel 25,000 miles in your car each year at an aver-age speed of 46 mph, you will spend approximately the same amount of time in your car as a college student does in an average year of class work. The question then becomes, What will you do with that time? Will you spend it listening to meaningless input or yelling at the driver next to you, or will you invest it in something that can dramatically change the results you are getting in life? These tapes can propel you to the success you are seeking. Don't try to learn the lessons of life slowly; learn from the masters who are willing to pass on the wisdom of the ages.

Abraham, Jay. *Your Secret Wealth*. Jay is an incredible thinker and innovator. He is a master at showing people how to use leverage and optimization to multiply their income.

Hill, Napoleon. *The Science of Personal Achievement*. A wonderful collection of original speeches given by the author of *Think and Grow Rich*.

Kiyosaki, Robert. *Rich Dad Secrets*. Secrets to money, business, and investing . . . and how you can profit from them.

Nightingale, Earl. *Lead the Field*. An old classic, used by thousands of salespeople.

Templeton, Sir John. *Laws of Inner Wealth*. Principles for spiritual and material abundance.

Tracy, Brian. *Getting Rich in America*. The best information I have found on starting your own business.

Tracy, Brian. *The Psychology of Selling*. The best compact training course in selling skills and techniques I have been able to find.

Tracy, Brian. *The Universal Laws of Success and Achievement*. Brian does a great job of overviewing the principles for success, happiness, and achievement.

Waitley, Denis. *The Psychology of Winning*. One of the best-selling tape sets of all time. Used to train Olympic athletes. How to *think* like a winner.

(Most of these tape/CD sets are available from *Nightingale Conant*. 1-800-323-5552 or at www.nightingale.com. Call for free catalogue of sales and motivational tapes.)

HELPFUL INTERNET SITES FOR JOB-HUNTING

The Internet provides a nearly unlimited amount of information on any subject. Careers are certainly no exception. You can research companies, post your résumé, review current job openings, explore your own business opportunities and plan your financial retirement—all on the Internet.

You may be thinking, *How can all this information really be of value if it is free?* Well, trust me, you will be exposed to a variety of advertising as you make you way around the Internet. However, the job-hunting information you will find is valuable and can save you an immense amount of time in preparing and planning your course of action.

Note of Caution: While the Internet is a helpful source of information, I do not recommend it as a quick cure for everything you need. Posting a résumé there is somewhat like dropping a few out of an airplane. Looking for a job online has the same challenges as seeing an ad in the newspaper: what you see is also seen by thousands of other job seekers. Seventy-five percent of companies that have hired over the Internet say they have had a bad experience. Hiring is still very much a nose-to-nose process. Use this to your advantage. Make personal contacts and find opportunities others won't find.

One other note: Internet addresses change with the wind. Even major organizations change sites quickly and often. If a link is not active, just move on. There are plenty to choose from.

Here are just a few of the sites we have found most helpful:

www.jobhuntersbible.com (This site has a constantly updated version of job-hunting on the Internet from the career guide *What Color Is Your Parachute?*)

www.careers.org (Lists over 11,000 links to jobs, employers, and business, education and career service professionals on the Web, plus 6,000 other helpful career resources. Includes how to post your resume, etc.)

TOP JOB BOARDS

www.monster.com
www.careerbuilder.com
www.hotjobs.com
www.flipdog.com
www.jobsearch.org
www.net-temps.com
www.vault.com
www.4jobs.com
www.employment911.com
www.nationjob.com
www.job.com
www.employmentguide.com
www.careersite.com
www.careerboard.com
www.directemployers.com
www.jobbankusa.com
www.topusajobs.com
www.wetfeet.com
www.coolworks.com
www.snagajob.com
www.careermag.com
www.truecareers.com
www.jobwarehouse.com
www.localcareers.com
www.preferredjobs.com
www.bestjobsusa.com
www.sologig.com
www.hiregate.com
www.jobfind.com
www.careershop.com
www.groovejob.com
www.career.com
www.summerjobs.com
www.employmentspot.com
www.americanjobs.com
www.4work.com
www.worklife.com

JOB POSTINGS

www.ajb.dni.us—maintained by the Department of Labor, US Employment Service (links 2,000 state employment service offices).

www.careerbuilder.com—features some 32,000 ads from 8 major newspapers in the US.

www.monstertrak.com—lists over 2,100 new job postings each day, primarily for college students, graduates, and alumni.

www.monster.com—just what it sounds like, a megacollection of more than 50,000 job listings. This site also has a personal search agent called Swoop which is free to job hunters.

www.careercity.com—lists virtual job fairs in dozens of cities. You can click on a city and then scroll through a number of employers' cyber-booths.

http://careers.excite.com/index.html?PG=home&SEC=feat—includes over 100,000 listings and a personal job-search agent.

www.careersonline.com.au/col/AskCOL.html—offers bilingual career aptitude testing, career design seminars, job search counseling, résumé preparation, and career counseling.

www.dice.com—a database for financial and technical areas of focus.

www.jobbankusa.com—provides employment networking and information services to job seekers, employers, and recruitment firms.

www.cooljobs.com—"cool" positions listed here.

http://tua.com/hom385/index.html—dream jobs to go. More on working on a cruise ship, being a dog groomer, etc.

CAREER COUNSELING ONLINE

http://guide-p.infoseek.com—give you a list of career centers on the Web.

http://jobsmart.org

www.union.edu—the Career Development Center at Union College.

www.myemploymentlawyer.com—for help with a legal question.

www.employmentreview.com—see where employment trends are going.

www.bls.gov—the latest US government figures regarding employment trends and issues.

www.workforce.com—employee and legal issues.

SALARIES

www.salary.com—the best overall salary site, complete with relocation calculator and a thorough list of career areas.

http://jobsmart.org/tools/salary/index.htm—a complete list of salaries on the Net.

http://stats.bls.gov/oco—find salary trends and the official "Occupational Outlook Handbook."

TALES FROM OTHER UNHAPPY WORKERS

http://disgruntled.com—site for unhappy people to tell their stories. Last year more than 800,000 people lost their jobs, and millions more are just not happy. (Note: There is a funny addendum to this. The editor of this site has resigned "because of an ongoing dispute over wages, benefits, and working conditions at this magazine."

www.yourefired.org—painful recollections of "winners who work for losers."

www.jobreference.com—place where someone can check your references.

INTERNET SITES FOR BUSINESS

SELF-EMPLOYMENT

www.workingsolo.com—lists 1,200 business resources for those seeking self-employment.

www.sbaonline.sba.gov—this US Small Business Administration site has a massive amount of information and lots of links.

www.nfibonline.com—a wonderful site by the National Federation of Independent Business, giving you daily information concerning legislation affecting small business and a great variety of daily tips for being more successful.

www.entrepreneurmag.com—find a business for sale, business building information, business opportunities, etc.

www.aahbb.org—the American Association of Home-Based Businesses

www.madetoorderwebsites.com—for an inexpensive Web site to start your business.

www.hoaa.com—the Home Office Association of America.

www.nationalbusiness.org—National Business Association.

http://nmbc.org—the National Minority Business Council.

www.soho.org—Small Office Home Office helps home-office professionals.

WOMEN WORKERS NETWORK NEWS

With the shift from a time-and-effort economy to a results-based economy, more women have discovered ways to leverage their abilities into corporate and entrepreneurial ventures. Want to network with other women? In addition to the organizations listed below, check with your local women's chamber of commerce and industry associations.

- National Association for Female Executives, (800) 634-NAFE, www.nafe.com
- National Association of Women Business Owners, (202) 347-8686, www.nawbo.org
- Women Business Enterprise National Council, (202) 872-5515, www.wbenc.org
- Women's Foodservice Forum, (312) 245-1047, www.womensfoodserviceforum.com

   (Source: *Entrepreneur*, November 2001)

COLLEGE-RELATED INTERNET SITES

You have seen my emphasis on personal skills and examples of people who have found their passion and ways to apply that without lots of traditional degrees. However, the options for getting formal degrees are becoming easier and more accessible. If you find you need additional training to pursue the work you love, you will be excited to know some new options.

EDUCATION OPTIONS

www.classesusa.com/featuredschools/fos/index.cfm?CFID=519076&CFTOKEN=91509819—the most comprehensive site I know for exploring distance education options.

http://info.universityofphoenixcampuses.com—the University of Phoenix is the best-known and most rapidly growing alternative education option.

www.jec.edu—JEC College Connection works with 12 universities, offering a choice of 200 classes and 11 degree programs. Classes are taught primarily through videotapes and the Internet.

www.tesc.edu—Thomas Edison State College offers bachelor's degrees in 119 majors; 14 degree programs can be completed entirely through distance learning.

www.lesko.com/help/EducationandTrainingHelp.htm—Matthew Lesko is a wild guy, but there is a ton of helpful and interesting information here. You'll enjoy it!

SCHOLARSHIP AND MONEY OPTIONS FOR SCHOOLING

The National Commission on Student Financial Assistance reports that of the $7 billion dollars available in scholarships to students in 2002, only $400 million was claimed.

The thought of searching through thousands of books and manuals may be a daunting prospect; however, the Internet just made your search process much easier.

Without leaving the comfort and familiarity of your own home, you can now have access to information on over 300,000 different forms of scholarships in a matter of seconds.

You may have been approached about different companies or individuals that offer the search process for a fee but can you do it on your own just as well? The answer is *yes*. The reason so much power and service is offered for free is that while you are searching, you will be shown many friendly advertisements from vendors and suppliers who would like your business. In exchange for this promotional exposure, you will be given powerful up-to-the-minute searches to legitimately help you find money. Many of the sites will actually prepare request letters for you.

The following is a brief sampling of URL addresses that will be helpful in the scholarship search process.

www.fastweb.com—the Internet's largest free scholarship search. Will search daily for over 375,000 different awards.

www.finaid.org—find out how to estimate financial need, sources of financial aid, scholarships, grants, contests, tuition payment plans, etc.

www.fdncenter.org—the Foundation Center's site for philanthropy and giving to those in need. You might fall into an interesting category that some foundation wants to give to.

www.scholarshipseminar.homestead.com—a site managed and updated by my friend Mike Turner, an expert on the scholarship process.

www.ets.org—has standardized test information, practice questions, and college searches.

www.collegeboard.com—the College Board site for online SAT registration, test dates, and college searches.

www.gocollege.com—find college scholarship searches and practice for the SAT and ACT.

www.yahoo.com/education/financial_aid—get access to college financial aid offices, sources of financial aid, grants, loans, and scholarship programs.

www.yahoo.com/education/higher_education—contains information about college and university academic competitions and honors programs.

www.fastaid.com

www.freschinfo.com

www.scholarsite.com

www.collegenet.com/mach25

www.finaid.org/scholarships/scams.phtml—how to avoid scholarship scams.

Recognize that this process does take time, but the results can provide a tremendous payback. Start at least 1 year in advance. The searches will go out each day and find new prospects for you. Then you must request the application forms and complete them.

Attitude
by Charles Swindoll

The longer I live, the more I realize the impact of attitude on life. Attitude, to me, is more important than the past, than education, than money, than circumstances, than failures, than successes, than what other people think or say or do.

It is more important than appearance, giftedness, or skill. It will make or break a company . . . a church . . . a home. The remarkable thing is we have a choice every day regarding the attitude we will embrace for that day.

We cannot change our past. . . . We cannot change the fact that people will act in a certain way. We cannot change the inevitable. The only thing we can do is play on the one string we have, and that is our attitude. . . .

I am convinced that life is 10 percent what happens to me and 90 percent how I react to it. And so it is with you. . . . We are in charge of our attitudes.

(Source: See http://zaadz.com/quotes/authors/charles_swindoll.)

Acres of Diamonds

Years ago, when the first diamonds were being discovered in Africa, diamond fever spread across the continent like wildfire. Many people struck it rich in their search for the sparkling beauties, and they became millionaires overnight.

At this time, Lamar, a young farmer in central Africa, was scratching out a moderate living on the land that he owned. However, the promise of great diamond wealth soon possessed Lamar, and one day he could no longer restrain his insatiable desire for diamonds and the lust to become a wealthy man. He sold his farm, packed a few essentials and left his family in search of the magnificent stones.

His search was long and painful. He wandered throughout the African continent, fighting insects and wild beasts. Sleeping in the elements, fighting the damp and cold, Lamar searched day after day, week after week, but found no diamonds. He became sick, penniless, and utterly discouraged. He felt there was nothing more to live for, so he threw himself in a raging river and drowned.

Meanwhile, back on the farm that Lamar had sold, the farmer who bought the land was working the soil one day and found a strange-looking stone in the small creek that ran across the farm. The farmer brought it in to his farmhouse and placed it on the fireplace mantle as a curio.

Later a visitor came to the farmer's home and noticed the unusual stone. He grasped the stone quickly and shouted excitedly at the farmer, "Do you know this is a diamond? It's one of the largest diamonds I've ever seen!" Further investigation revealed that the entire farm was covered with magnificent diamonds. In fact, this farm turned out to be the site of one of the richest and most productive diamond mines in the world, and the farmer became one of the wealthiest men in Africa.

How sad that Lamar had not taken the time to investigate what he had right at his own fingertips. Instead, he gave up everything he had to search for wealth that was available to him right under his nose. The seeds of opportunity are usually in what we already know about and are already doing. Don't think "the grass is greener on the other side of the fence" or that you must start something totally new and different to become successful. Just do what you already know 10 percent better or provide added value.

TAKEAWAYS

1. You have more options than you may have realized. When we look at changing work models, you realize you can not only choose a company, but you can choose how you want to relate to that or any company.

2. You can embrace who you are even if you want to do something independently.

3. If you know how to put a plan together, you can benefit from all the ideas you have been accumulating all your life.

REFLECTIONS ON WORK MATERIALS

1. Review "Acres of Diamonds". Sometimes the best options are right under our noses.

2. Are you comfortable with the idea that we are just returning to the kind of businesses our country was founded on?

3. Review the frequently asked business start-up questions. Do these make a business seem more attractive?

4. Are you a candidate for considering work options outside of the traditional "employee" model?

5. Review the helpful Internet sites. It's not the magic solution to anything, we still need the nose-to-nose contact for success, but it does help in gathering information.

ASSIGNMENTS FOR NEXT WEEK

1. Find yourself on the *48 Days* schedule and continue on to completion.

2. Begin your job search contacts.

3. Keep track of your ideas by writing them down and creating plans of action.

4. Begin the next chapter of a fulfilling life!

The Business Source Marketplace

CAREER PLANNING PERSONALITY STYLE ANALYSIS

A 35-page personalized computer report which will clearly define your own personality strengths and weaknesses, your value to an organization, how you are best motivated, how you communicate, and in what environment you work best. In the best-selling book *Financial Peace*, author Dave Ramsey says, "Everyone has some natural talent or aptitude in one or more areas. If you can identify those areas you not only will be happier and perform more successfully in that role, but you will also become better paid for that. . . .This is such an important financial concept that I recommend detailed aptitude testing if you are not happy and functioning at peak efficiency."

Career Planning Profile: $75.00
Discount price: $37.50
www.48days.com/products.php

48 DAYS TO CREATIVE INCOME®
BY DAN MILLER

Do you have a desire to own your own business, but haven't a clue how to get it off the ground? Are you wondering how you can generate extra income? Do you have an idea? A patent? An invention? Do you have a service to offer you feel sure would be successful? In this workbook and CD set, you will learn how to determine if you have the right personality to be an "eaglepreneur"®. Also included is how to get started, how to choose a product or service, sales and marketing essentials, how to develop your idea or product, etc. A must for anyone considering doing something nontraditional!

48 Days To Creative Income® Workbook with two Audio CDs: $49.00
Check site for current specials: www.48days.com/products.php

IS YOUR JOB YOUR CALLING?®
BY DAN MILLER

This 35-minute CD gives you insight into why "planning your work around the life you want" is essential to overall career success. To do this you must first understand who you are and make the process one of life planning! Is Your Job Your Calling is a message of hope to those of you who are still struggling with what you want to be when you grow up.

Is Your Job Your Calling?® Audio CD: $11.00

Contact us at:

The Business Source, P. O. Box 681381 Franklin, TN 37068-1381
Order online at our Web site where you will see more products,
current workshop and teleseminar schedules, and free reports!
www.48days.com

Notes